W9-CPE-831

The Green
Movement

Peggy J. Parks

Energy and the Environment

ReferencePoint
Press®

San Diego, CA

© 2012 ReferencePoint Press, Inc.
Printed in the United States

For more information, contact:
ReferencePoint Press, Inc.
PO Box 27779
San Diego, CA 92198
www.ReferencePointPress.com

Picture credits:
Cover: iStockphoto.com
Maury Aaseng: 31–33, 46–47, 61–63, 75–77
AP Images: 72
© Aaron M. Cohen/Corbis: 9

LIBRARY OF CONGRESS CATALOGING-IN-PUBLICATION DATA

Parks, Peggy J., 1951–
   The green movement / by Peggy J. Parks.
     p. cm. — (Compact research series)
   Includes bibliographical references and index.
   ISBN-13: 978-1-60152-163-7 (hardback)
   ISBN-10: 1-60152-163-4 (hardback)
   1. Green movement. 2. Environmentalism. I. Title.
   JA75.8.P36   2012
   320.5'8—dc23
                                         2011023719

Contents

Foreword

As modern civilization continues to evolve, its ability to create, store, distribute, and access information expands exponentially. The explosion of information from all media continues to increase at a phenomenal rate. By 2020 some experts predict the worldwide information base will double every 73 days. While access to diverse sources of information and perspectives is paramount to any democratic society, information alone cannot help people gain knowledge and understanding. Information must be organized and presented clearly and succinctly in order to be understood. The challenge in the digital age becomes not the creation of information, but how best to sort, organize, enhance, and present information.

ReferencePoint Press developed the *Compact Research* series with this challenge of the information age in mind. More than any other subject area today, researching current issues can yield vast, diverse, and unqualified information that can be intimidating and overwhelming for even the most advanced and motivated researcher. The *Compact Research* series offers a compact, relevant, intelligent, and conveniently organized collection of information covering a variety of current topics ranging from illegal immigration and deforestation to diseases such as anorexia and meningitis.

The series focuses on three types of information: objective single-author narratives, opinion-based primary source quotations, and facts and statistics. The clearly written objective narratives provide context and reliable background information. Primary source quotes are carefully selected and cited, exposing the reader to differing points of view. And facts and statistics sections aid the reader in evaluating perspectives. Presenting these key types of information creates a richer, more balanced learning experience.

For better understanding and convenience, the series enhances information by organizing it into narrower topics and adding design features that make it easy for a reader to identify desired content. For example, in *Compact Research: Illegal Immigration*, a chapter covering the economic impact of illegal immigration has an objective narrative explaining the various ways the economy is impacted, a balanced section of numerous primary source quotes on the topic, followed by facts and full-color illustrations to encourage evaluation of contrasting perspectives.

The ancient Roman philosopher Lucius Annaeus Seneca wrote, "It is quality rather than quantity that matters." More than just a collection of content, the *Compact Research* series is simply committed to creating, finding, organizing, and presenting the most relevant and appropriate amount of information on a current topic in a user-friendly style that invites, intrigues, and fosters understanding.

The Green Movement at a Glance

Green Movement Defined

The green movement is made up of large and small environmental organizations, grassroots groups, and private individuals; their agendas may differ, but the common bond they share is a desire to protect and preserve the environment.

Roots of the Green Movement

Environmentalism has existed for more than a century, but many attribute the birth of the modern green movement to the first Earth Day, which took place on April 22, 1970.

Core Issues

Some of the green movement's major priorities include air and water pollution, toxic waste, wilderness preservation, protection of wildlife habitats and endangered species, sustainability, and climate change.

Effects on Environmental Policies

The green movement, especially in its first two decades, influenced Congress to pass nearly 30 major environmental initiatives and has played a major role in strengthening environmental policies over the years.

Ecoterrorism

Groups such as the Earth Liberation Front are known for using violence to prevent environmental destruction, so the FBI has labeled them ecoterrorists.

Benefits Versus Costs of Going Green

Growing numbers of companies are implementing practices that allow them to save money while causing less damage to the environment; most consumers are interested in purchasing greener products, but most do not want to pay substantially more.

Greenwashing

Some companies that advertise their products as green are merely using that label as a marketing tool rather than actually following practices that benefit the environment.

The Future

The green movement's focus in the future will be on trying to regain public enthusiasm that was prolific during the 1970s and 1980s by convincing people that environmental issues are still an important concern.

Overview

> **The diverse and eclectic 'Green movement' can name some of the century's most passionate, selfless and ultimately foresighted people amongst its ranks.**
>
> —Michael Buick, director of the United Kingdom–based emission trading company, Sandbag.

> **We're constantly urged to 'go green'—use less energy, shrink our carbon footprint, save the Earth. How? We should drive less, use ethanol, recycle plastic and buy things with the government's Energy Star label. But what if much of going green is just bunk?**
>
> —John Stossel, a conservative columnist and political commentator.

On April 22, 2010, a celebration took place in cities and towns throughout the United States and in nearly 200 other countries. It was the fortieth anniversary of Earth Day, an environmental event that was founded in 1970 by the late US senator Gaylord Nelson. An environmental activist for many years, Nelson was disturbed by what he perceived as a callous disregard for the planet, and he had become frustrated over politicians' seeming lack of interest in environmental issues. So, he came up with the idea of holding a national "teach-in" that was modeled after peaceful Vietnam antiwar demonstrations.

As enthusiastic as he was about the event, Nelson could never have anticipated the millions of people from all walks of life who would get involved. Nor could he have known that Earth Day 1970 would become one of the largest grassroots demonstrations in US history. "That day left a permanent impact on the politics of America," he later wrote.

A crowd gathers on the National Mall in Washington, DC, in April 2010 to celebrate the fortieth anniversary of Earth Day, an annual event that highlights issues of environmental quality and resource conservation. Earth Day has been described as helping to launch the modern green movement.

It forcibly thrust the issue of environmental quality and resources conservation into the political dialogue of the Nation. That was the important objective and achievement of Earth Day. It showed the political and opinion leadership of the country that the people cared, that they were ready for political action, that the politicians had better get ready, too. In short, Earth Day launched the Environmental decade with a bang.[1]

What Is the Green Movement?

For decades, major movements have played a vital role in effecting change for the betterment of society. Although each of these movements had its own individual focus, they can all be summed up in two words: people power. The green movement is no exception. Composed of an eclectic mix of large and small organizations, grassroots groups, and private individuals, the green movement represents the collective power of people. Their specific agendas may differ, but all who are part of the green movement share a common goal: protecting and preserving the health and vitality of the planet.

> "Composed of an eclectic mix of large and small organizations, grassroots groups, and private individuals, the green movement represents the collective power of people."

Green movement efforts have led to cleaner lakes, rivers, and streams; safer drinking water; and air that is no longer choked with toxic industrial pollutants. Wildlife habitats have been restored, numerous forests and parks are protected under federal and state laws, and many endangered species are no longer threatened by human actions. Even with this progress, many environmental concerns still exist. Wangari Maathai, an activist and author from Kenya, Africa, describes the importance of green movement efforts when she writes: "While a certain tree, forest, or mountain itself may not be holy, the life-sustaining services it provides—the oxygen we breathe, the water we drink—are what make existence possible, and so deserve our respect. From this point of view, the environment becomes sacred, because to destroy what is essential for life is to destroy life itself."[2]

Nineteenth-Century Roots

Scottish-born naturalist and conservationist John Muir described a similar spiritual connection to the environment more than a century ago. During the mid-1800s Muir explored places of natural beauty such as California's Sierra Nevada mountain range, the Grand Canyon, the Petrified Forest, and Yosemite Valley. Referring to Yosemite, Muir wrote that it was "by far the grandest of all the special temples of Nature I was ever permitted to enter."[3] Through his travels, Muir became convinced that these wild and natural places needed the protection of the federal government. He played a major role in convincing President Theodore Roosevelt to enact conservation programs that created the first national monuments and national parks. In 1892 Muir and some of his supporters founded the Sierra Club to help create awareness of the importance of protecting America's unspoiled beauty.

Another nineteenth-century advocate of the environment was philosopher and writer Henry David Thoreau, and he, too, viewed it in a spiritual way. During the mid-1800s Thoreau published a series of essays and books about the ties between humans and nature, in which he urged people to appreciate and conserve the natural environment. Sonoma State University emeritus professor of sociology David Walls writes: "When Henry David Thoreau left Concord in 1845 to write and study nature for two years at [Walden] Pond, he became the harbinger of twentieth century conservationists who would preserve the natural world for its beauty and potential for spiritual enlightenment, not merely for its practical value."[4]

> **The publicity generated by *Silent Spring* fueled public outrage and sparked a renewed passion for the importance of preserving and protecting the environment.**

An "Explosion of Activism"

Although seeds of environmentalism were sown in the nineteenth century, that was also a time of rampant environmental degradation. During the Industrial Revolution, which began in Britain in the 1850s and then spread to the United States, manufacturing flourished, with factories springing up one after another, their smokestacks spewing noxious emissions into the air. Waterways became choked with pollution, as industrial operations located on the banks of rivers and lakes disposed of toxic waste by dumping it into the water. In the absence of environmental regulation, flagrant pollution of the air, water, and land continued unabated well into the twentieth century.

A turning point came in 1962, when Rachel Carson released a book called *Silent Spring*. An environmental scientist from Springdale, Pennsylvania, Carson was aware of nature's delicate balance, and she had be-

Crews clean up oil-soaked straw on a Santa Barbara, California, beach in 1969. An oil spill off the Santa Barbara coast galvanized environmentalists, who helped pressure Congress into passing a variety of bills tackling air and water pollution, garbage, and protections for marine animals and endangered species.

come convinced that humans were altering that balance—in some cases, irreversibly. Carson wrote about how widespread use of the pesticide DDT was hurting predatory bird populations, who were accumulating large amounts through their food sources. This accumulation resulted in thinner eggshells that collapsed under the weight of the adult birds, killing the chicks and drastically reducing their populations. Carson used her book to sound the alarm about the potential long-term effects of pesticides before the sounds of nature were silenced.

The publicity generated by *Silent Spring* fueled public outrage and sparked a renewed passion for the importance of preserving and protecting the environment, as the Sierra Club writes: "[Carson's] work shook the prevailing view of humankind's place in the web of life, and called for us to take responsibility for the preservation of the Earth's diversity. Her words helped shape the environmental movement as we know it today."[5]

Nelson shared Carson's concerns for the environment and found two incidents to be especially disturbing. One was a January 1969 accident at an oil rig off the coast of Santa Barbara, California. Due to a series of mishaps, more than 200,000 gallons (750,000L) of crude oil spread over 800 square miles (2,072 square km) of ocean, killing tens of thousands of seabirds and untold numbers of fish and other marine creatures. The second incident happened five months later in Cleveland, Ohio. The Cuyahoga River, which empties into Lake Erie, had become a dumping site for toxic waste from steel mills and other industries along the riverbank. On June 22, 1969, when sparks from a passing train landed on oil- and chemical-soaked debris, the river burst into flames. Although the fire burned for less than a half hour before being extinguished, the Cuyahoga became a national symbol for how rivers and lakes throughout the United States were being poisoned.

> " In modern society, the ways in which people use energy, manufacture products, grow crops, dispose of waste, and in general, live their lives, can adversely affect the environment. But with sustainability as a goal, threats to the planet can be minimized. "

By the time Earth Day was held a year later, the American people were demanding change—and they got it. Walls writes: "In 1965 there were no more than a half-dozen national conservation organizations with citizen members and some degree of influence, and most were on a shaky financial footing. Although conservationists were beginning to win important victories preserving wilderness and protecting air and water from pollution, no one anticipated the explosion of activism that was about to take place."[6]

A Focus on Sustainability

In recent years, "sustainability" has become synonymous with the green movement. Groups such as the United Nations Environment Programme have suggested various definitions for the word, but its simplest meaning is for natural resources to be used in such a way that they are not depleted and the environment is not harmed. The Aquinas College Center for Sustainability uses an analogy to illustrate the basic concept of sustainability: "What does an ant colony need to sustain itself? It needs access to fresh water, clean air to breathe, healthy food, and a suitable location for the colony. The natural world has supplied these necessities to the ants and the only waste produced is a fertilizer for the soil. Therefore, the ant colony is an example of a sustainable society."[7]

The concept of sustainability is much more complex when it is applied to humans. In modern society, the ways in which people use energy, manufacture products, grow crops, dispose of waste, and in general, live their lives, can adversely affect the environment. But with sustainability as a goal, threats to the planet can be minimized, as environmental journalist and author Bryan Walsh explains: "As we learn to develop smarter, we can help avoid some of those problems—in fact, sustainable development is really at the heart of environmentalism today, as we attempt as a species to manage natural resources and grow without choking the planet."[8]

How Has the Green Movement Influenced Environmental Policies?

In the years since the green movement formed, it has proved to have a significant effect on environmental protection. Tom Burack, commissioner of the New Hampshire Department of Environmental Services, writes: "I would argue that being green has been woven into our daily lives, and taking actions that are beneficial to our environment is accepted and encouraged, and is helping to create a better future. This is certainly in stark contrast to the state of our environment on that first Earth Day in 1970."[9]

Just six months after the first Earth Day, the Environmental Protection Agency (EPA) opened in Washington, DC. While its creation may not have been the direct result of green movement efforts, the movement can be credited with the massive increase in public pressure that forced the government to address environmental protection issues. This led to Congress's passage of more than 30 environmental initiatives during the 1970s, including the Clean Air Act, the Clean Water Act, the Endangered Species Act, the Safe Drinking Water Act, and the Toxic Substances Control Act, as well as amendments that strengthened existing environmental policies.

Greening Communities

The influence of the green movement is increasingly visible in the growing number of communities that are adopting green practices. One example is Vancouver, a city in the Canadian province of British Columbia, which was named the greenest city in Canada and is also considered one of the greenest cities in the world. A citizen-led movement called Village Vancouver is working toward making the city even greener than it already is, with a goal for Vancouver to become an example for other communities worldwide. Says the group's founder, Ross Moster: "I tend to think we're only limited by our imagination."[10]

Just a few hours away from Vancouver is Seattle, Washington, which is also known for being green. On more than one occasion, Seattle has been recognized by the Natural Resources Defense Council (NRDC), an influential environmental action group based in New York City. In March 2011 Seattle received the highest ranking on the NRDC's list of the top 15 greenest large cities in America. The group evaluated such factors as standard of living, air and water quality, recycling and waste reduction efforts, and energy production/conservation. One of many reasons Seattle received the designation was that its energy provider, Seattle City Light, is the first US utility company to achieve net zero greenhouse gas emissions status, and it has made the commitment to satisfy all future growth with conservation and renewable energy.

Green, Greener, Greenest

A strong indication that the green movement has gotten its message across is the numerous businesses and corporations that have implemented green policies to guide their day-to-day operations. Some, such as Dell Computer, have achieved worldwide recognition for superior green efforts. Long known for being an environmentally friendly company, Dell was rated number one in *Newsweek* magazine's 2010 Top 100

> **The influence of the green movement is increasingly visible in the growing number of communities that are adopting green practices.**

Greenest Companies in America. One of its green efforts is designing desktop and laptop computers that consume 25 percent less energy than those produced in 2008, which saved its customers an estimated $5 billion in energy costs over the past few years.

Another major commitment on Dell's part is offering free recycling of its products worldwide and banning the export of electronic waste to developing countries, a practice that has been identified as one of the fastest-growing and most dangerous environmental problems. A March 2011 article in *Going Green Today* explains:

> According to the EPA, the US generated over 3 million tons of e-waste in 2008 with less than a 14% recycling rate. Dell Reconnects is a partnership with Goodwill that provides 2200 sites to collect electronic products from any manufacturer. These electronics are filled not only with hazardous, but also valuable and scarce materials—everything from lead to cadmium to mercury.[11]

Johnson & Johnson is also a green trendsetter, ranking fifth in Forbes's 2010 top 10 list of America's Greenest Companies. A major reason Johnson & Johnson earned this distinction is that nearly 40 percent of its energy comes from renewable sources such as solar, wind, and biomass. The company has set aggressive goals for sustainability and environmental protection, including increasing reliance on renewable energy and energy savings, reducing its water consumption, vastly cutting down on carbon dioxide emissions, and significantly reducing hazardous and nonhazardous waste.

True Green Versus Greenwashing

With the green movement's emphasis on greener business policies, practices, and products, many companies are feeling pressured to prove that they fit the green profile. And while hundreds of these companies are indeed committed to fulfilling their green promises, numerous others have used misleading or deceptive marketing efforts to portray themselves as more eco-conscious than they actually are. Sustainability marketing manager Mike Kapalko writes: "With another company claiming to be 'green' seemingly every day, it's becoming more difficult to decipher what's real and what's hype."[12]

This "hype" is known as greenwashing, and according to the environmental consulting firm TerraChoice the practice is widespread. A report released by the group in October 2010 shows that since 2009, the number of "greener" products has gone up by 73 percent. But after evaluating nearly 5,300 consumer products, all of which made an environmental claim, the findings were sobering: Of all these products, 95 percent were either not green at all or fell short of being as green as the

> **With the green movement's emphasis on greener business policies, practices, and products, many companies are feeling pressured to prove that they fit the green profile.**

manufacturers claimed—and this included 100 percent of the toys and 99.2 percent of the baby products that were surveyed by the group. As the report states: "If 'green' demand is to create genuinely 'greener' products, the environmental claims of those products must be true and transparent. This is why greenwashing is such a significant impediment to continued progress."[13]

Do the Benefits of Going Green Outweigh the Costs?

Since a major focus of the green movement is encouraging private citizens, groups, and companies to adopt greener lifestyles and business practices, the benefits of going green versus the cost of doing so are often debated. Green products are typically higher priced, and consumers are not always willing to pay the extra cost. This became evident during an October 2010 survey by the market research group Crowd Science, in which only 14 percent of respondents said they would pay "substantially more" for products that were better for the environment.

Businesses must also give serious consideration to the cost of going green versus the potential benefits. Although numerous companies have adopted greener policies and procedures, and are convinced that doing so will help them be more efficient and therefore profitable, others are not necessarily convinced that going green pays off. This was apparent in a June 2010 survey by the public relations firm Gibbs & Soell, in which 78 percent of executives said the primary obstacle to more businesses going green was insufficient return on investment.

What Is the Future of the Green Movement?

Since the 1970s the green movement has made immense progress, from spearheading environmental regulation and cleanup efforts to influencing companies and individuals to adopt greener ways of living and doing business. Its future, however, is not so well defined. Some are convinced that the movement has lost its momentum and lacks a clear vision for where it needs to go in the future. Referring to its failure to influence Congress to pass legislation that would cap greenhouse gases and curb global warming, Walsh writes: "Accustomed to remaining optimistic in the face of long odds, the environmental movement all at once faces a challenge just to stay relevant in a hostile political climate."[14]

> " Many hope that these younger leaders can breathe new life into the green movement, figure out how to recapture lost momentum, and continue to build on that. "

One of the ways the green movement is generating renewed enthusiasm for its cause is through younger leadership, as environmentalist and *Earth Island Journal* editor Jason Mark writes: "For the first time in a generation, a number of significant green groups are led by people under 40." Groups that are now led by people in their twenties and thirties include Greenpeace USA, Friends of the Earth, Rainforest Action Network, Sierra Club, and the international climate justice group 350.org. Many hope that these younger leaders can breathe new life into the green movement, figure out how to recapture lost momentum, and continue to build on that. Mark explains: "If the warnings about Earth's terminal health are accurate, then it is not an overstatement to say that the wealth of our civilization depends in large measure on the ability of a cohort of twenty- and thirty-somethings to succeed where their predecessors fell short."[15]

Looking Ahead

From the dreams of John Muir and Henry David Thoreau more than a century ago to today's growing emphasis on the importance on adopting greener lifestyles, the green movement has made its presence known. Whether it can continue to remain influential in the coming years may be a matter of uncertainty, but one fact cannot be denied—in one way or another, the green movement's impact on the world has been profound. Environmental writer and editor Larry West shares his thoughts: "It's safe to say that environmentalism has become a powerful force in American culture and politics. Ongoing efforts to understand more clearly how we can use natural resources without depleting them, and enjoy natural beauty without destroying it, is inspiring many of us to take a more sustainable approach to the way we live and to tread a little more lightly on the planet."[16]

What Is the Green Movement?

❝Living green is not something that can be prescribed or bought. It is a varied practice that is both old and new, that includes high-tech innovations and long held traditions.❞

—Jennifer Rosket and Laura Mamo, sociologists and researchers who cofounded the group Social Green.

❝We have spent a huge amount of time talking about polar bears and melting ice caps, but unless we can connect those events to things immediate to people's lives, then behaviour change simply won't last.❞

—Ben West, the communications coordinator at the UK Youth Climate Coalition.

Although she is only 18 years old, Ally Maize has already proved that she is a green leader. Her passion for environmental issues began to develop when she was a freshman in high school, as she writes: "I was starting to become addicted to learning more about all of the air, water, and land pollution that is causing so many environmental problems on this planet. . . . Since that time, I have spent countless hours learning as much as I can on the subject."[17] For Maize, it was not enough to merely live a greener lifestyle herself—she wanted to do something bigger, something that would allow her to inspire and motivate other young people to embrace the green cause. So, she founded her own nonprofit organization called the Green Youth Movement.

In the three years since Maize's dream became reality, Green Youth Movement membership has soared, and she has become known as Los Angeles's "Green Teen." Her group has planted sustainable gardens at schools and private homes and partnered with other green organizations such as the Million Trees Project in Los Angeles. In October 2010 the Green Youth Movement sponsored the Green Initiative Humanitarian Fashion Show in Hollywood, which featured clothing by designers known for using only sustainable materials and environmentally responsible production methods. Yet even with all that she has done, Maize has even bigger dreams for the future. She intends for the Green Youth Movement to keep growing, to become better known, and to get the message across to young people that they have the power and ability to change the world "one kid at a time."[18]

Toward a More Sustainable World

Over the years the green movement has increasingly focused on sustainability, which is often defined as meeting the needs of the present without compromising the ability of future generations to meet their needs. Peter Senge, who is a senior lecturer in behavior and policy science at the Massachusetts Institute of Technology, writes: "For me, sustainability means paying attention to very fundamental needs—food, water, energy, and the waste and toxicity they produce. . . . What we're talking about is arguably the greatest challenge to innovation that humankind has ever faced: reinventing our whole way of living." According to Senge, "sustainability" and "future" are inextricably linked. He explains: "You just ask, what's the world of your children and grandchildren going to be like? What would you like to see it be like? Do you have a sense of giving them a world that's in better shape than your parents and grandparents gave you?"[19]

To illustrate his point about the link between sustainability and the future, Senge refers to a meeting that took place between a group of young people and educational administra-

> **Over the years the green movement has increasingly focused on sustainability, which is often defined as meeting the needs of the present without compromising the ability of future generations to meet their needs.**

tors. He says that he will never forget one particular conversation in which a 12-year-old girl was discussing how those of older generations were using up the earth's resources without considering what might be left in the future for younger people. Speaking to the president of the American Superintendents Association, she said, "You know, we kind of figure like you drank your water and then you drank ours."[20]

According to Senge, one example of true sustainability is manufacturers considering the entire life cycle of their products, which is often called the cradle-to-grave philosophy. "What's becoming clearer to companies is what happens to stuff after you make it," he says.

> In Europe today, you make a car, you have to take it back at the end of its lifetime. That's the law. Same is true for a lot of consumer electronics. That's a fundamental shift in a business model. A few companies in Europe led the charge to design those regulations and they became world leaders of design for remanufacture and design for recycling. If you design the car right, you can have a lot of value in it even when it's no longer efficient to operate.[21]

Sustainability is an issue of importance for Alice Marcus Krieg, who owns a thriving horticulture business in the New York City borough of Brooklyn. She says that people often do not realize how sustainability is woven into the lifestyles of New York residents. "Sustainability begins with decisions on how best to live," she says. "It's about much more than carrying cloth bags to the food market—it's a choice on how best to use your resources for better living." She adds that the focus on sustainability "has changed NYC into a city where the focus is not on industry growth, but more on quality of life." A prime example of this concept is the numerous New York restaurants that specialize in serving locally grown food purchased only from upstate farmers. "New York is an agricultural state, one of the first actually," says Marcus Krieg. "So sustainability was really born here."[22]

The Big (Green) Apple

New York's commitment to being a greener, more sustainable city is obvious in a number of ways, as Marcus Krieg writes: "This city is all about space management. Living here forces you to constantly make decisions about how best to use the space, as we're all so crammed in. Every inch is considered." She refers to New York's urban planning, which has changed dramatically over the past 15 years and is now focused on making public spaces both attractive and sustainable. "Traffic patterns have been diverted to allow for plantings and new public plazas," she says. "Due to new traffic patterns on the streets, bike lanes have been incorporated. Old railroad tracks, historically elevated to bring goods from the Hudson River to warehouses, are being turned into public parks via public and private partnerships. These parks offer extremely diverse plantings, and native species are incorporated into parks so that what was here originally exists again."[23]

Because of the time, effort, and commitment New York City's leaders have devoted to greening the city, their actions have captured the attention of environmental groups. For instance, the Natural Resources Defense Council (NRDC) has included New York in its list of the 22 greenest "Smarter Cities" for the past two years. The group's recognition of New York in 2011 was in the transportation category for its mass transit system, as well as its plans to create 60 miles (96.7km) of additional bicycle lanes.

> " **Because of the time, effort, and commitment New York City's leaders have devoted to greening the city, their actions have captured the attention of environmental groups.** "

In 2010 New York was recognized in the energy category for developing innovative and effective conservation programs that have reduced the demand for energy. Because of what the NRDC refers to as "New York's sea of rooftops,"[24] city leadership has long been aware of the vast potential for installing solar panels to generate power. In conjunction with the Solar American Cities Initiative, which is funded by the US Department of Energy, the city is studying ways that solar energy can be expanded. Another area of intense study is the possibility of tapping into the energy of tides and currents. Experts say that if this energy could be harnessed, 3,000 megawatts of electricity could potentially be generated—enough to power more than a million households.

The Changing Face of Agriculture

One focus of environmental groups over the years has been the agriculture industry. Agriculture consumes immense amounts of energy and natural resources and is a major source of land and water pollution from fertilizers, pesticides, and animal waste. According to the National Sustainable Agriculture Coalition, agriculture is the largest source of pollution in rivers and streams, affecting roughly half of total stream miles. The group writes: "Over 100 million acres of cropland still erode at unsustainable levels, despite decades of soil conservation efforts stemming back to the Dust Bowl. Nearly two-thirds of threatened and endangered species are listed due in some part to agriculture and agro-chemicals."[25]

> Each year, food producers (including farmers) as well as business leaders and others who are committed to sustainable food systems are honored by the Natural Resources Defense Council with Growing Green Awards.

The many problems associated with agriculture, along with society's heightened demand for healthier, fresher, chemical-free foods, have led to the growth of smaller-scale agriculture and organic farming. Bryan Walsh writes: "There are now thousands of community-supported agriculture programs around the country, up from just two in 1986. There are more than 6,000 farmers' markets, up 16% from just a year ago. Sales of organic food and beverages hit nearly $25 billion in 2009, up from $1 billion in 1990, and no less a corporate behemoth than Walmart has muscled into the organic industry, seeking out sustainable suppliers."[26]

Some leading green groups have embraced the cause of sustainable agriculture. Journalist and food activist Michael Pollan says that these groups

have come to appreciate that a diversified, sustainable agriculture—which can sequester large amounts of carbon in the soil—holds the potential not just to mitigate but actually to help solve environmental problems, including climate change. Today, environmental organizations like the

Natural Resources Defense Council and the Environmental Working Group are taking up the cause of food system reform, lending their expertise and clout to the movement.[27]

Each year, food producers (including farmers) as well as business leaders and others who are committed to sustainable food systems are honored by the Natural Resources Defense Council with Growing Green Awards. One of the winners in 2011 in the food producer category was Jim Cochran, the owner of Swanton Berry Farm in Santa Cruz, California, who was one of the state's first organic strawberry farmers.

Along with strawberries, Cochran grows blackberries, kiwis, artichokes, and a number of other vegetables without using any chemical pesticides or fumigants to control weeds. He chose to become an organic farmer in 1981, when he was poisoned by pesticides that had been sprayed overnight. "This was when it was becoming obvious that pesticides were way more harmful than people had been led to believe,"[28] he says. Although it took several years to convert his farming practices to organic, and he initially lost money, Cochran is now one of the most profitable strawberry producers in the United States. He says that the NRDC Growing Green Award "is a milestone for our industry . . . an award not just for Swanton Berry Farm or myself, but for an entire generation of people who have been doing their best to follow a truly holistic vision of sustainability."[29]

> **Of the numerous groups and organizations that make up the green movement, the majority advocate peaceful solutions to addressing environmental problems—but the same cannot be said for extremist groups whose actions are anything *but* peaceful.**

Dangerous Greens

Of the numerous groups and organizations that make up the green movement, the majority advocate peaceful solutions to addressing environmental problems—but the same cannot be said for extremist groups whose actions are anything *but* peaceful. In fact, some are so extreme in their tactics that the Federal Bureau of Investigation (FBI) has labeled them "ecoterrorists." The Anti-Defamation League (ADL) Law Enforcement Agency Resource Network explains: "In recent years, fast-food restaurants have been firebombed and car dealerships and housing developments burned to the ground in the name of 'ecology' and 'animal rights.' Increasingly, people that work for companies perceived as harming animals or destroying the environment are targeted as well."[30]

One of the most notorious green extremist groups is the Earth Liberation Front (ELF), which is dedicated to ending environmental destruction. According to the ADL's Law Enforcement Agency Resource Network, ELF activists typically try to accomplish their goals "by causing damage to the operations of companies in related industries or terrorizing executives and employees of these and associated companies."[31] In April 2010 an ELF member was sentenced to five years in prison for attempting to burn down a multi-million-dollar condominium development in Pasadena, California. According to the FBI, Steven James Murphy installed a gasoline bomb in a partially constructed condo unit in September 2006. Before leaving the scene Murphy set a timer so the bomb would explode later, but the device failed to ignite. Arson investigators said that if the bomb had functioned as Murphy planned, the explosion would have been powerful enough to destroy the entire development and possibly surrounding structures as well.

A Movement with a Mission

From greener cities to sustainable agriculture, the green movement has made an indelible mark on the world. Not everyone subscribes to the green philosophy, and those who do often have very different attitudes about what it means to be green, as well as how "sustainability" is defined. Yet for everyone who is passionate about protecting the planet and embraces what the green movement stands for, living green becomes more important every day.

What Is the Green Movement?

66 The environmental movement is perhaps the most significant contemporary global movement to have emerged in recent decades. 99

—Liam Leonard and John Barry, eds., *Global Ecological Politics*. Bingley, Emerald Group, 2010.

Leonard is with the Institute of Technology in Sligo, Ireland, and Barry is with Queen's University in Belfast, Northern Ireland.

66 At best, the green movement might be compared to an alarm clock: jangling shrilly to wake up the world. 99

—Walter Russell Mead, "The Big Green Lie Exposed," *American Interest*, July 12, 2010. http://blogs.the-american-interest.com.

Mead is senior fellow for US foreign policy at the Council on Foreign Relations and a leading expert on American foreign policy.

* Editor's Note: While the definition of a primary source can be narrowly or broadly defined, for the purposes of Compact Research, a primary source consists of: 1) results of original research presented by an organization or researcher; 2) eyewitness accounts of events, personal experience, or work experience; 3) first-person editorials offering pundits' opinions; 4) government officials presenting political plans and/or policies; 5) representatives of organizations presenting testimony or policy.

Primary Source Quotes

> **❝This is the root of too much of modern environmental thinking: Humanity is an interloper in a pristine, peaceful world.❞**

—*Washington Times*, "Arbor Day vs. Earth Day," editorial, May 5, 2009. www.washingtontimes.com.

The *Washington Times* is a general interest daily newspaper based in Washington, DC.

> **❝We're consuming resources and polluting the planet at a level the Earth cannot sustain.❞**

—BioRegional, "One Planet Living," 2011. www.bioregional.com.

With offices in the United Kingdom, South Africa, China, and North America, BioRegional seeks to help businesses, governments, and individuals to live and work more sustainably.

> **❝Instead of counting the ways in which we have harmed the planet, we should be focusing on how to improve it. And contrary to what greens might believe, the best way to do that today is to promote human prosperity.❞**

—Alex B. Berezow, "Earth Day Goal Should Be Human Prosperity," Real Clear Science, April 20, 2011. www.realclearscience.com.

Berezow holds a PhD in microbiology and is the editor of the online science-focused publication Real Clear Science.

> **❝'Green' is a pretty big circus tent under which any number of efficient, renewable, sustainable, environmental, recyclable ideas can comfortably fit.❞**

—Amy Foster Parish, "What Does 'Green' Mean?," Microsoft Hohm Community Blog, June 28, 2010. http://blog.microsoft-hohm.com.

Parish is an energy specialist at the Washington State University Extension Energy Program.

❝People don't like feeling guilty, and we already know that the green movement comes with a heavy load of guilt.❞

—Graceann Bennett and Freya Williams, "Mainstream Green," *The Red Papers*, Ogilvy & Mather, April 2011. www.ogilvyearth.com.

Bennett is managing partner and director of strategic planning at Chicago's Ogilvy & Mather, and Williams is cofounder and head of strategy at OgilvyEarth.

❝We live in a time when the phrase 'green building' doesn't indicate paint color. Our president has encouraged green jobs and clean energy, and CEOs pose for glamour shots in architecturally designed, sustainable buildings.❞

—Gregory Fairchild, "When Innovation Is a Risk for Small Businesses," *Washington Post*, February 5, 2011. www.washingtonpost.com.

Fairchild is executive director of the Tayloe Murphy Center and associate professor of business administration at the University of Virginia's Darden School of Business.

❝Different actors have long had different motives for pursuing environmental protection and conservation, and some of those motives have been at odds.❞

—Kjell Nilsson et al., eds., *Forests, Trees and Human Health*. New York: Springer, 2010.

Nilsson is head of the Division of Parks and Urban Landscapes at the University of Copenhagen in Denmark.

What Is the Green Movement?

- In a March 2011 Gallup poll, participants were asked about their role in the environmental movement; **20 percent** said they were active participants, **42 percent** said they were sympathetic but not active, **27 percent** were neutral, and **9 percent** were unsympathetic.

- According to a 2010 report by the environmental consulting firm TerraChoice, between 2009 and 2010 the number of green product offerings increased **73 percent**.

- Of more than 2,300 adults who participated in a November 2010 survey by Harris Interactive, **75 percent** at least somewhat agreed with the statement "I am green."

- Of more than 2,300 Americans who participated in a November 2010 Harris Interactive survey, **83 percent** said environmental issues were at least somewhat important when considering which products or services to purchase.

- An **environmental scorecard** released in August 2010 by the Natural Resources Defense Council ranked four cities not typically considered green among the highest for their environmental and conservation efforts: New York City; Reno, Nevada; Columbus, Ohio; and Dubuque, Iowa.

Many Businesses Not Perceived as Green

The green movement has had an impact on many facets of society, including companies that have implemented greener practices and introduced green products. Yet according to an April 2011 poll, most consumers and Fortune 1000 executives believe that only *some* businesses are committed to going green, rather than *most*.

In your opinion, how many businesses are committed to "going green"—that is, improving the health of the environment by implementing more sustainable practices and/or offering environmentally friendly products or services?

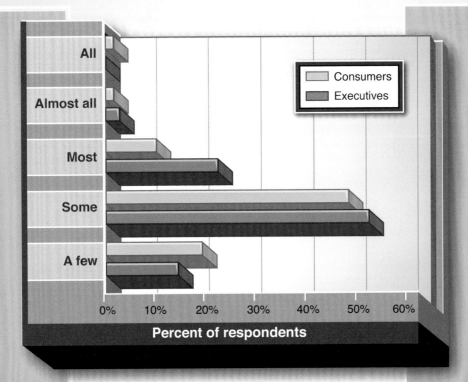

Source: Gibbs & Soell, *2011 Gibbs & Soell Sense and Sustainability Study*, April 2011. www.gibbs-soell.com.

- According to the Federal Bureau of Investigation, ecoterrorist groups have been responsible for over **2,000 crimes** and over **$110 million** in economic losses since 1979.

Steady Growth of Recycling

In the years since the green movement formed, one of its priorities has been to encourage individuals and businesses to recycle in order to reduce the amount of waste that ends up in landfills. There has been significant progress in this endeavor since 1960.

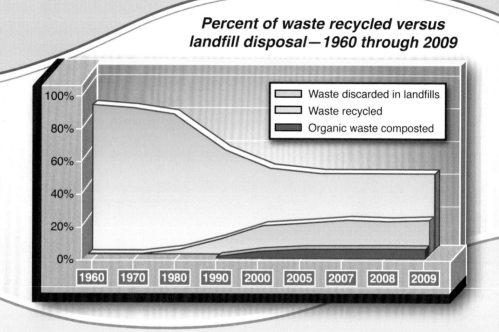

Percent of waste recycled versus landfill disposal—1960 through 2009

Legend:
- Waste discarded in landfills
- Waste recycled
- Organic waste composted

Y-axis: 100%, 80%, 60%, 40%, 20%, 0%

X-axis: 1960, 1970, 1980, 1990, 2000, 2005, 2007, 2008, 2009

Source: U.S. Environmental Protection Agency, *Municipal Solid Waste in the United States: 2009 Facts and Figures,* December 2010. www.epa.gov.

- In a June 2010 survey by the public relations firm Gibbs & Soell, **33 percent** of executives from companies with fewer than 500 employees and **36 percent** of executives from companies with 500 to 1,000 employees said their businesses had a team of individuals who worked on "going green" initiatives in addition to their primary job descriptions.

Pollution Still Considered a Problem

In 1970, when the first Earth Day launched the modern green movement, pollution of the land, air, and water was rampant in the United States. Over the years progress has been made in cleaning up the environment and curbing pollution. Yet according to a May 2010 survey by Virginia Commonwealth University, most Americans still view air and water pollution as major problems and are also concerned about other environmental issues.

Does this represent a major problem for the country, a minor problem, or not a problem at all for the country today?

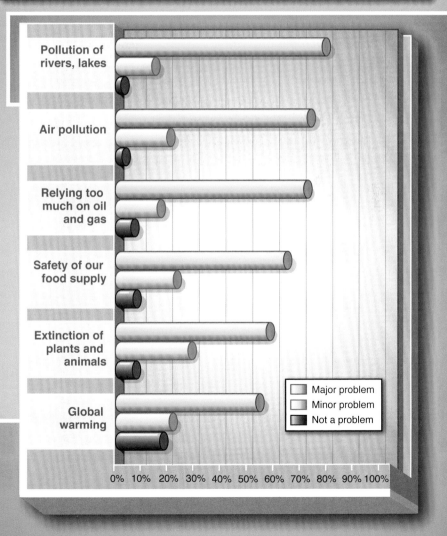

Note: Responses not indicated here were "Don't know."

Source: Virginia Commonwealth University, *VCU Life Sciences Survey 2010*, May 27, 2010. www.vcu.edu.

33

- Of more than 1,000 participants in an April 2010 survey by the Boston-based strategy and communications agency Cone, **67 percent** reported being confused by the messages companies use to talk about their social and environmental commitments.

- In an April 2011 report by the Chicago advertising, marketing, and strategy organization Ogilvy & Mather, **68 percent** of American respondents thought it was important to take public transportation, bicycle, or walk to work, but only **27 percent** actually did; of Chinese respondents, **93 percent** thought it was important and **84 percent** did.

- Although the green movement has made substantial progress in curbing pollution, in a May 2010 survey by Virginia Commonwealth University, **80 percent** of participants viewed the pollution of rivers and lakes as a serious environmental problem, and 74 percent felt that way about air pollution.

- In an April 2011 survey by Rasmussen Reports, only **38 percent** of respondents thought the annual Earth Day celebration has helped raise environmental awareness.

- Between 2008 and 2009 the percentage of Americans who told the Pew Research Center for the People and the Press that the environment was a top priority declined from **56 percent** to **41 percent**.

How Has the Green Movement Influenced Environmental Policies?

> **The 'green' movement has had a great impact on world trade and government policy.**
>
> —Omar Espinoza and Brian Bond of the Department of Wood Sciences and Forest Products at Virginia Tech University.

> **Environmentalists attempt to move public opinion, they don't set public policy.**
>
> —Adam Werbach, former president of the Sierra Club and the author of *Strategy for Sustainability: A Business Manifesto*.

I f one symbol represents how the collective power of the green movement has influenced environmental protection, it is the transformation of Ohio's Cuyahoga River. Once a murky, oily, garbage-choked body of water where not even leeches or sludge worms could survive, the Cuyahoga is now teeming with fish and has been designated a state scenic river. Its banks are home to diverse wildlife, including beavers, river otters, and spotted turtles, as well as nesting sites for great blue herons. Because of the numerous species of fish in the river, it has become the ideal habitat for eagles to feed and nest. In 2007, for the first time in over

70 years, a pair of bald eagles nested on the riverbank and fledged their young. "It's a miracle," says Cleveland resident Gene Roberts, an avid fisherman who vividly remembers the sordid condition of the Cuyahoga four decades ago. "The river has come back to life."[32]

An "Avalanche" of Environmental Laws

After the infamous Cuyahoga River fire in 1969, the publicity it generated proved to be a major catalyst for the growth of the green movement. As the US National Park Service explains, "it helped spur an avalanche of pollution control activities."[33] The launching point was a bill known as the National Environmental Policy Act (NEPA), which was drafted by Congress in December 1969 and signed into law on New Year's Day by then-president Richard M. Nixon. NEPA established a broad national framework for environmental protection and was the first piece of legislation to do so. Its basic premise was to ensure that all branches of government give proper consideration to the environment prior to undertaking any major action that could significantly affect it.

> After the infamous Cuyahoga River fire in 1969, the publicity it generated proved to be a major catalyst for the growth of the green movement.

NEPA became the foundation for a decade of environmental policies and was hailed by Gaylord Nelson as "the most important piece of environmental legislation in our history." Nelson added that it "came about in response to the same public pressure which later produced Earth Day."[34] By the end of 1970 the Environmental Protection Agency (EPA) opened in Washington, DC, and America's "environmental watchdog" was vested with a vast amount of regulatory power. The EPA was charged with establishing and enforcing environmental protection standards, conducting research, and making recommendations to the president for new environmental protection policies. Since the EPA represented everything the green movement stood for, in many ways it acted as the movement's governmental arm.

Soon after its inception, the EPA began taking aggressive steps to reverse environmental damage. The first major law was the Clean Air Act, which went into effect on December 31, 1970. An article on EPA's history touts the importance of the legislation: "The Clean Air Act brought dramatic—and substantive—changes to the federal air quality program. The act required EPA to establish national air quality standards as well as national standards for significant new pollution sources and for all facilities emitting hazardous substances." The article adds that one of the EPA's first actions under the Clean Air Act was to take "dead aim against America's leading source of pollution: the automobile. The law set statutory deadlines for reducing automobile emission levels: 90 percent reductions in hydrocarbon and carbon monoxide levels by 1975 and a 90 percent reduction in nitrogen oxides by 1976."[35]

Taking Aim at Acid Rain

The initial priority for the Clean Air Act was to curb air pollution that was harming human health, but during the late 1970s another mysterious environmental problem was starting to capture scientists' attention. They observed that lakes, rivers, and streams in the northeastern United States were steadily growing more acidic, which was killing off aquatic life. In the Adirondacks, a mountain range in northern New York State, an estimated one-quarter of the 3,000 lakes and streams had become too acidic to support fish. Washington University atmospheric chemist Dan Jaffe, who grew up in the Boston area, noticed this at a young age and spent time talking with fishermen around New England. "All these old-timers kept telling me the lakes had been full of fish that were now gone,"[36] says Jaffe.

To investigate this problem, Congress passed the Acid Deposition Act in 1980, which called for the funding of a 10-year research program. When the study was complete, the researchers concluded that the environmental damage was indeed significant and was being caused by acid rain. A phenomenon first identified in the late nineteenth century, acid rain forms when sulfur dioxide and nitrogen oxides

> Since the EPA represented everything the green movement stood for, in many ways it acted as the movement's governmental arm.

are emitted into the atmosphere, primarily by coal-burning power plants but also by other industrial operations and vehicles. When the pollutants are absorbed by water droplets in clouds, a chemical reaction occurs in which the toxins are changed into sulfuric and nitric acids. The acids then fall to the earth in the form of precipitation such as rain, snow, or sleet, which alters the chemistry and biology of lakes, streams, and rivers. The researchers who performed the study also found that in addition to killing aquatic life, acid rain was destroying forests in the Adirondacks and Appalachian Mountains. This was caused by acidic soil, as well as acid-laden fog that bathed high-elevation trees in acids and stripped their leaves of nutrients.

> "Along with federal legislation, green movement efforts have led to environmental protection laws passed at the state and local levels."

Based on study findings, the Clean Air Act was amended in 1990 to include acid rain. This gave the EPA the authority to require power plants to significantly reduce emissions of sulfur dioxide and nitrogen oxides, which the agency accomplished by implementing a program known as cap and trade. Industries were given a maximum allowance (a cap) of pollutants that they were allowed to emit into the air. If they reduced their emissions faster than the law required, they could bank the excess allowances for future use or sell them to other industries. According to an article on the EPA's *Greenversations* blog, in the years since the acid rain program has been in place, sulfur dioxide emissions have dropped 63 percent, and nitrogen dioxide emissions have dropped 70 percent. In March 2010 the EPA proposed legislation that would decrease these emissions even more.

Regional Green Action

Along with federal legislation, green movement efforts have led to environmental protection laws passed at the state and local levels. The Sierra Club, for instance, has been working with citizens in Massachusetts to pass H. 2614, an act designed to phase out coal-fired electric generation by the year 2020. This largely came about because serious air pollution in the state has been shown to contribute to its high rate of asthma, including nearly 135,000 children who suffer from the disease. James McCaffrey, director of the Massachusetts Sierra Club, explains:

> Massachusetts is the only New England state that still relies significantly on coal-fired power plants. . . . People nationwide are abandoning this outdated source of electricity and moving to clean, reliable sources of energy that don't make their families sick. We can do better than coal by promoting safe and renewable alternatives which, in turn, will create long term job opportunities for Massachusetts residents.[37]

Green movement efforts have also been involved in the fight against coal pollution in Chicago. For more than 10 years, residents and environmental groups have been demanding that the utility company reduce emissions from its Fisk coal-fired power plant, which was built in the early 1900s and has not been updated for more than 50 years. A city ordinance mandating major cuts in sulfur dioxide and nitrogen oxide emissions was introduced in 2001 but never adopted. In the last few years, Greenpeace and more than 50 other groups have organized thousands of Chicago residents to demand passage of a new piece of legislation called the Clean Power Ordinance, which is again designed to regulate power plant emissions.

Out of frustration over a perceived lack of action, on May 24, 2011, eight Greenpeace activists climbed the plant's 450-foot smokestack (137m) and painted "QUIT COAL" in giant letters down the length of it. One of them, Kelly Mitchell, stated to the news media: "As a Chicago resident, I know that we must shut this plant down—to make our air cleaner, our communities safer, and to stop the effects of global warming. All across America, companies like Edison International are poisoning communities with their coal plants—people like us are fighting to have those communities voices heard."[38] Activists vowed to keep fighting to get the aging power plant shut down, converted to natural gas, or modernized with pollution control equipment that would significantly reduce toxic emissions.

Greens Losing Ground?

The green movement in the United States grew stronger and increasingly influential during the 1970s and 1980s because environmental damage was so blatant. Signs of this were most everywhere, from rivers and lakes that had been turned into sewers to severe damage caused by acid rain. The public was justifiably outraged and pressured legislators to pass laws that would protect the environment and punish industries that were flagrant polluters. Today, the green movement still works toward keeping those policies in place, as well as strengthening existing laws so the air, water, and land will be pollution free. But one of its major focuses in recent years—legislation that would help stop global warming—is an area where the green movement has made little or no headway.

> **Because of its inability to convince legislators of the importance of climate change policy, the green movement has been sharply criticized, with some people wondering if the movement itself is losing ground that it will never be able to regain.**

Although global warming is a controversial issue, many scientists warn that the earth is heating up at a far more rapid rate than would occur under natural circumstances. This, they are convinced, is being caused by human activities, especially the burning of fossil fuels such as coal. One particularly outspoken believer in global warming is Bill Gates, the founder of Microsoft. With a personal fortune estimated at $50 billion, Gates has invested millions of dollars of his own money to help curb global warming by creating other sources of carbon-free energy. He explains: "Climate change is a terrible problem, and it absolutely needs to be solved. It deserves to be a huge priority."[39] Yet it has not been treated as a priority in the United States, which lags behind many other industrialized countries in enacting climate change policies—and Congress has shown no signs that this will change anytime soon.

Because of its inability to convince legislators of the importance of climate change policy, the green movement has been sharply criticized, with some people wondering if the movement itself is losing ground that it will never be able to regain. "What went wrong?" asks *New Republic* associate editor Bradford Plumer. "For months now, environmentalists have been asking themselves that question, and it's easy to see why. After Barack Obama vaulted into the White House in 2008, it really did look like the United States was, at long last, going to do something about global warming."[40] Plumer refers to the numerous scientists who were united in the global warming cause, as well as green groups that seemed to be making inroads in getting cap and trade legislation passed to reduce carbon emissions. He refers to the latter as "a total flop," saying that the green movement is "even further from solving climate change than we were in 2008."[41]

Not everyone is convinced, however, that the green movement has failed in this endeavor. Plumer refers to his interview with David Hawkins, who is director of climate programs at the Natural Resources Defense Council. According to Hawkins, setbacks have always been a factor in how much the green movement could achieve, and climate change legislation is no exception. "It's not the sort of conclusion that's going to grab headlines," says Plumer. "But that doesn't mean he's wrong."[42] In the meantime, green movement advocates plan to keep fighting for policies that will curb global warming in the same way legislation has addressed numerous other environmental problems.

Challenges Ahead

Innumerable environmental laws and policies can be traced back to green movement influence. The air is fit to breathe, rivers and lakes are cleaner, and forests are no longer being wiped out by acid rain. Groups such as the Sierra Club and Greenpeace have aided citizens and other groups seeking an end to pollution from coal-fired power plants and other sources. Still, there is a long way to go and much work to be done before all environmental problems are a thing of the past. When that time will come—or if it is even possible—is unknown.

How Has the Green Movement Influenced Environmental Policies?

66 Recent debate over environmental policy has been shaped by these right-wing promulgators of sound-bite philosophies that are blithely indifferent to science, reason, or the public good. 99

—Denis Hayes, "Radical Elements Sway Courts, Undercut Environmental Protections," Earth Day Network, April 25, 2011. www.earthday.org.

Hayes is an environmental lawyer and chief executive officer of the Bullitt Foundation, an environmental organization located in Seattle, Washington.

66 Virtually everyone on the left has thrown on the green pants, green shirts, and green cloak of what we are assured is the future of life on earth as we know it. 99

—Kenneth P. Green, "The Myth of Green Energy Jobs: The European Experience," *Energy and Environment Outlook*, February 2011. www.aei.org.

Green is a resident scholar at the American Enterprise Institute for Public Policy Research.

* Editor's Note: While the definition of a primary source can be narrowly or broadly defined, for the purposes of Compact Research, a primary source consists of: 1) results of original research presented by an organization or researcher; 2) eyewitness accounts of events, personal experience, or work experience; 3) first-person editorials offering pundits' opinions; 4) government officials presenting political plans and/or policies; 5) representatives of organizations presenting testimony or policy.

66 Shifting subsidies to the development of climate be-
nign energy sources such as wind, solar, and geothermal power will help stabilize the earth's climate. 99

—Lester Brown, *World on the Edge: How to Prevent Environmental and Economic Collapse*. New York: WW Norton, 2011.

Brown is founder and president of the Earth Policy Institute and former president of Worldwatch Institute.

66 Not only are the sprouts of environmental reform vig-
orous but they are also breaking through the pavement
in corporate America of all places. Big companies that
for a long time hid behind Washington's failure to act
are now getting out ahead—because cleaning up their
act is good business. 99

—Carl Pope, "Green Sprouts in the Sidewalk?," *Huffington Post*, March 11, 2011. www.huffingtonpost.com.

Pope is chairman of the Sierra Club.

66 American environmentalists must develop new un-
derstandings of their own and humanity's place on
earth, and translate that understanding into political
practice. 99

—Paul Wapner, *Living Through the End of Nature: The Future of American Environmentalism*. Cambridge, MA: MIT Press, 2010.

Wapner is associate professor and director of the Global Environmental Politics
Program in the School of International Service at American University in Washington, DC.

66 Much has been made in the news media about the green
movement and the profound effects it will have on the
business world and the everyday marketplace. 99

—Peter Sander and John Slatter, *The 100 Best Stocks You Can Buy*. Avon, MA: Adams Business, 2009.

Sander is a researcher and personal finance/business consultant, and Slatter is
an independent investment adviser.

> **The reason that the Great Global Green Dream is melting lies in the sad truth that whatever the scientific facts of the matter, the global green movement is so blind and inept when it comes to policy and process that it has deeply damaged the causes it cares most about.**

—Walter Russell Mead, "The Big Green Lie Exposed," *American Interest*, July 12, 2010. http://blogs.the-american-interest.com.

Mead is senior fellow for US foreign policy at the Council on Foreign Relations and a leading expert on American foreign policy.

> **Green has now moved into the mainstream, reconfiguring the playing field for businesses large and small. Whereas attention to environmental issues has to this point been largely mandated through regulation, the new reality is that green initiatives are increasingly market driven.**

—Jim L. Bowyer, "The Green Movement and the Forest Products Industry," *Doors and Hardware*, October 2009.

Bowyer is professor emeritus in the Department of Bioproducts and Biosystems Engineering at the University of Minnesota, St. Paul.

Facts and Illustrations

How Has the Green Movement Influenced Environmental Policies?

- The Clean Air Acts of 1970, 1977, and 1990 gave the EPA the authority to reduce the presence of six **atmospheric pollutants** to meet national health standards: lead, sulfur dioxide, carbon monoxide, nitrogen oxides, ozone (smog), and particulates (soot).

- The EPA states that in 2010 alone reduction in fine particle and ozone pollution from the 1990 Clean Air Act amendments prevented more than 160,000 cases of **premature death**, 130,000 **heart attacks**, and 1.7 million **asthma attacks**.

- Of more than 1,000 people who participated in an April 2010 survey by the strategy and communications agency Cone, **92 percent** said collaboration between business, government, and organizations to solve social and environmental issues was either very or somewhat important.

- Since the **Clean Air Act** was amended in 1990 to include acid rain, sulfur dioxide emissions have been reduced by over 5.5 million tons (4.99 million metric tons).

- In a June 2011 Gallup/*USA Today* poll, participants were asked if they favored or opposed regulating energy from private companies in an attempt to reduce global warming; **56 percent** favored it, and **40 percent** were opposed.

Green Legislation Passed in the Seventies

The formation of the green movement is largely attributed to the first Earth Day, which was held in 1970. Within six months of that first Earth Day, the Environmental Protection Agency (EPA) opened in Washington, DC, and Congress passed numerous environmental laws during the 1970s.

Legislation	Year Enacted	Description
Clean Air Act	1970	Regulated air emissions from stationary and mobile sources; authorized the EPA to establish the National Ambient Air Quality Standards to protect public health and public welfare, and to regulate emission of hazardous air pollutants.
Clean Water Act	1972	Strengthened and expanded the Federal Water Pollution Control Act of 1949; established the basic structure for regulating discharges of pollutants into water in the United States and regulating quality standards for surface waters.
Endangered Species Act	1973	Charged the US Fish and Wildlife Service and the US National Oceanic and Atmospheric Administration Fisheries Service with providing for the conservation of threatened and endangered plants and animals and the habitats in which they are found.
Safe Drinking Water Act	1974	Protected the quality of drinking water in the United States by focusing on all waters actually or potentially designed for drinking use, whether from above-ground or underground sources.
Toxic Substances Control Act	1976	Provided the EPA with the authority to enforce reporting, record-keeping and testing requirements and restrictions related to chemical substances and/or mixtures.

Source: Environmental Protection Agency, "Historical Topics," May 13, 2011. www.epa.gov.

US Government Is Not Doing Enough

Many laws inspired by the green movement are in place to protect the environment but Americans mostly still believe that the US government is doing too little when it comes to environmental protection. Although public opinion on this question has fluctuated over time, a March 2011 Gallup poll shows that views have remained fairly steady between 1992 and 2011.

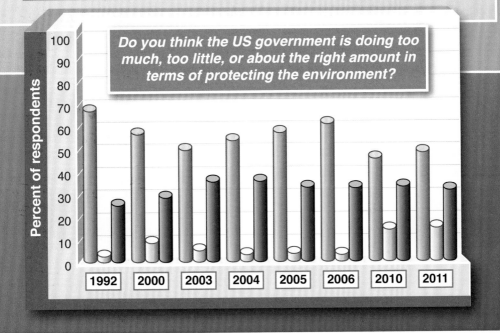

Do you think the US government is doing too much, too little, or about the right amount in terms of protecting the environment?

Percent of respondents

Too little   Too much   About the right amount

Source: Gallup, "Environment," March 17, 2011. www.gallup.com.

- In a June 2010 joint poll by Pew Research and the National Journal Congressional Connection, **56 percent** of respondents said protecting the environment was a higher priority for US energy policy than keeping energy prices low.

- In 1993 Portland, Oregon, became the first local government in the United States to adopt a **climate action plan** to help fight global warming.

- The corporation Johnson & Johnson has implemented aggressive energy policies, with nearly **40 percent** of its energy coming from renewable sources such as solar, wind, and biomass.

- In a March 2011 Gallup poll, **49 percent** of participants said they felt the US government was doing too little to protect the environment, **33 percent** said the amount was about right, and only **16 percent** said too much was being done.

- In an April 2010 survey by the strategy and communications agency Cone, **70 percent** of respondents said they would be willing to help influence corporate social and environmental policies by participating in surveys and research, and **44 percent** said they would accomplish this through boycotting a company's products.

- In May 2009 the 21st Century Green High-Performing Public Schools Facilities Act allocated **$6.4 million** for green projects such as energy-efficient modernization and renovation of schools throughout the United States.

- Of 1,300 consumers who participated in an October 2010 survey by the market research group Crowd Science, **47 percent** disagreed with the statement, "It makes no difference whether a company follows 'green'/eco-friendly practices."

Do the Benefits of Going Green Outweigh the Costs?

> 66 The green movement has created a new niche market of consumers who are highly concerned about the environment and are willing to do and spend more to be environmentally friendly. 99
>
> —Jeff Rogut, executive director of the Australian Centre for Retail Studies.

> 66 At the very least, the perception out there is that it takes green to be green. There is a prevailing belief among the masses that they are being excluded from the green movement because they simply aren't rich or cool enough to participate. 99
>
> —Graceann Bennett, managing partner and director of strategic planning at Chicago's Ogilvy & Mather, and Freya Williams, cofounder and head of strategy at OgilvyEarth.

As the chief executive officer of Xerox Corporation, Ursula M. Burns has an immense amount of responsibility, the most important of which is meeting the needs of customers and shareholders. Like all corporate executives, Burns is well aware that in a struggling economy every expense is scrutinized, and it is not uncommon for "social responsibility" budgets to be cut. She finds this disturbing, as she writes: "The thing is, what I do at my job and how I do my part for the environment are not mutually exclusive. 'Green' is not a corporate function housed in a separate unit devoted to social responsibility; green solutions and sustainable strategies are smart business—for everyone."[43]

Burns thinks it might be time for businesses to rethink the way they look at environmental responsibility, focusing on how going green is not only the right thing to do but also a way for a company to be more profitable. "The greener we get, the more we can reduce costs and boost efficiency," she says. "The more we reduce costs, the more productive a business can become and the better we can weather the maladies of the global business market."[44] Burns says that this strategy has worked at Xerox: In 2006 the company saved $18 million because of efforts to reduce greenhouse gases. She has seen the same thing happen at numerous other corporations that are also saving millions of dollars per year while reducing their environmental impact. "Now is not the time to cut investment in green technology and environmentally beneficial business practices," she writes. "No, now is the time to keep those investments that deliver a real, measurable return—where your business, your customers, and the world in which we live can reap the reward."[45]

> " Surveys have shown that doubts about whether going green is affordable are still common among many business professionals. "

Roadblocks to Green

Burns speaks from the perspective of someone who is at the helm of a Fortune 500 company and has seen firsthand how going green can benefit the environment as well as business. Numerous companies share her views, such as Dell Computer, Johnson & Johnson, and other green corporate trendsetters. Yet surveys have shown that doubts about whether going green is affordable are still common among many business professionals. For instance, in a June 2010 survey by the public relations firm Gibbs & Soell, only 29 percent of executives believed that a majority of businesses were committed to green practices. When they were asked to share their opinions about why this was the case, the two top reasons given were consumers' unwillingness to pay more for green products/services and insufficient return on investment.

Why businesses choose to become more environmentally focused—or choose not to—was the subject of an August 2010 *Wall Street Journal* article by University of Michigan strategy professor Aneel Karnani. According to Karnani, the perception that the primary motivation for companies to adopt greener business practices is a sense of responsibility or the desire to "do good" is flawed. Even though that tends to be a popular assumption, he says that the *real* driving force is profitability. He writes:

> Very simply, in cases where private profits and public interests are aligned, the idea of corporate social responsibility is irrelevant: Companies that simply do everything they can to boost profits will end up increasing social welfare. In circumstances in which profits and social welfare are in direct opposition, an appeal to corporate social responsibility will almost always be ineffective, because executives are unlikely to act voluntarily in the public interest and against shareholder interests.[46]

Karnani cites examples that are often touted to show how greener companies can be more profitable. Fast-food restaurants, for instance, have profited by expanding their offerings to include salads and other healthier options that appeal to health-conscious customers, and auto manufacturers have profited from responding to consumer demand for more fuel-efficient vehicles. "But social welfare isn't the driving force behind these trends," says Karnani.

> Healthier foods and more fuel-efficient vehicles didn't become so common until they became profitable for their makers. . . . These companies are benefiting society while acting in their own interests; social activists urging them to change their ways had little impact. It is the relentless maximization of profits, not a commitment to social responsibility, that has proved to be a boon to the public in these cases.[47]

Deep Green Deceit

Karnani notes that when executives are hired, their primary job is to maximize profits. Although they are vested with a massive amount of responsibility, including analyzing how their company can become greener, the bottom line is still in their hands—and it is what matters the most. "Even if executives wanted to forgo some profit to benefit society, they could expect to lose their jobs if they tried—and be replaced by managers who would restore profit as the top priority." Executives, expected to focus on profitability while under pressure to make the company greener, are in a difficult situation as Karnani writes: "That's one reason so many companies talk a great deal about social responsibility but do nothing—a tactic known as greenwashing."[48]

> " The severity of the greenwashing problem was revealed in the October 2010 TerraChoice report, which showed a 73 percent increase in so-called green products during 2009. But when evaluating more than 5,300 of these products, the group found that 95 percent had at least one green claim that was misleading or false. "

The term *greenwashing* traces back to the 1980s, when New York biologist Jay Westerveld was staying at a hotel. He noticed a small plastic sign that said "Save our planet," with verbiage suggesting that patrons re-use their towels rather than leave them on the floor to be washed. Westerveld was convinced that the hotel was using the message to sell itself as a green business, when in fact its goal was to save money and increase profits by using less water. Thus, he made up a word to describe the hotel's deceptive practice: *greenwashing*. "The word 'greenwashing' just came to me," he says. "It seemed really logical, pretty simple, kind of like whitewashing."[49] Since then, Westerveld has observed that greenwashing has become more prevalent and that the word *green* is often hijacked by companies that have no real commitment to the environment. "The meaning has been usurped," he says, "and it's not really about making the planet greener anymore."[50]

The severity of the greenwashing problem was revealed in the October 2010 TerraChoice report, which showed a 73 percent increase in so-called green products during 2009. But when evaluating more than

5,300 of these products, the group found that 95 percent had at least one green claim that was misleading or false. Scott McDougall, TerraChoice's chief executive officer, shares his thoughts: "If we allow companies to get away with exaggeration, consumer skepticism will become cynicism and they'll stop choosing green products at all."[51]

In January 2011 the US Federal Trade Commission (FTC) won a major victory against a greenwashing company called Tested Green. According to the FTC, the company charged hundreds of dollars for worthless green product certifications and made false claims to more than 100 companies. In marketing materials and on its website, Tested Green had called itself the "nation's leading certification program" and claimed to have made over 45,000 green product certifications in the United States. Says David Vladeck,

> **With the heavy push for going green, people are often given the message that making the lifestyle changes that will preserve and protect the planet is up to them. Inherent in these messages is a sense of guilt, which can be counterproductive.**

who is director of the FTC's Bureau of Consumer Protection: "It's really tough for most people to know whether green or environmental claims are credible. Legitimate seals and certifications are a useful tool that can help consumers choose where to place their trust and how to spend their money. The FTC will continue to weed out deceptive seals and certifications like the one in this case."[52]

Misplaced Responsibility

With the heavy push for going green, people are often given the message that making the lifestyle changes that will preserve and protect the planet is up to them. Inherent in these messages is a sense of guilt, which can be counterproductive. As the Ogilvy & Mather report states: "Much of our motivation for positive change has been unwisely based on [the] negative message of, 'What will happen if we don't act now?' As research has shown, this doom and gloom drive by those trying hardest to mobilize positive change has the unfortunate effect of inducing paralysis and skepticism, emotions only fostered by the array of confusing and contradictory media coverage."[53]

Another problem, according to environmental activist and author Derrick Jensen, is that when people are pressured to go green, they are often misled about how much of a difference they can actually make. He explains:

> Let's talk water. We so often hear that the world is running out of water. People are dying from lack of water. Rivers are dewatered from lack of water. Because of this we need to take shorter showers. See the disconnect? *Because I take showers, I'm responsible for drawing down aquifers?* Well, no. More than 90 percent of the water used by humans is used by agriculture and industry. The remaining 10 percent is split between municipalities and actual living breathing individual humans.[54]

To further make his point, Jensen references the movie *An Inconvenient Truth*, which was created by former vice president Al Gore to educate people about global warming. Jensen writes: "But did you notice that all of the solutions presented had to do with personal consumption—changing light bulbs, inflating tires, driving half as much—and had nothing to do with shifting power away from corporations, or stopping the growth economy that is destroying the planet?"[55]

Jensen makes it clear that he is not discouraging people from living greener lives or doing their part to help the environment—far from it. He just wants them to see the bigger picture, to understand that while individuals can collectively make a positive difference by going green, the bulk of the responsibility belongs with the industrial, agribusiness, commercial, government, and military sectors. For instance, more than 90 percent of water use is gobbled up by agriculture and industry, with the remaining 10 percent split between municipalities and individuals. Less than 25 percent of energy is used by private individuals, and only about 3 percent of the total waste stream is generated by municipalities. Jensen quotes environmentalist and author Kirkpatrick Sale, who offers this: "The whole individualist what-you-can-do-to-save-the-earth guilt trip is a myth. We, as individuals, are not creating the crises, and we can't solve them."[56]

Green *and* Quality

Studies have increasingly shown that people care about the environment and want to do their part by purchasing green products, which has led to growing demand. According to a report released in March 2010 by the market research firm Mintel, the green market grew by 41 percent from 2004 to 2009. The same report showed that more than one-third of consumers would be willing to pay more for green products. But in the Ogilvy & Mather survey, people made it clear that quality was equally important to them when they purchased these products. The report states: "Consumers demand an acceptable level of effectiveness for products, sustainable or not."[57]

Another commonality among consumers is their tendency to be loyal to their regular brands, which means they will rarely buy products that are unfamiliar just because they are labeled "green." When consumers who participated in the Ogilvy & Mather survey were asked if they would rather purchase the environmentally responsible product line from a mainstream brand with which they are familiar, or purchase a product from a company that specializes in being green and environmentally responsible, 73 percent opted for the known brand.

> " Another commonality among consumers is their tendency to be loyal to their regular brands, which means they will rarely buy products that are unfamiliar just because they are labeled 'green.' "

According to environmental strategist Joel Makower, for most people to choose a greener way of living, they must be convinced that doing so has tangible benefits—in other words, they must perceive *greener* as *better*. He writes:

> Most committed green consumers, I suspect, go with the faith-based notion that "green" equals "good"—or, at least, "good enough." But many mainstream consumers believe that "green" equals "*worse*"—that making environmentally responsible shopping choices means making a sac-

rifice in quality, affordability, convenience, or some other attribute. A relative few are willing to make such sacrifices in the name of a healthier planet or a better world. But not many are. And they won't do so until green = better.[58]

Room for Improvement

Few would disagree that making changes on behalf of the environment is a good thing to do. But studies show that challenges often get in the way of going green, from businesses concerned about cost versus profitability to consumers being skeptical about whether green products are really green. As companies feel increasingly pressured to get greener, many are making claims that are misleading or downright deceptive, with consumers bearing the brunt of greenwashing. If these problems could be resolved so that *green* is always associated with *better*, everyone would benefit.

Do the Benefits of Going Green Outweigh the Costs?

❝In circumstances in which profits and social welfare are in direct opposition, an appeal to corporate social responsibility will almost always be ineffective, because executives are unlikely to act voluntarily in the public interest and against shareholder interests.❞

—Aneel Karnani, "The Case Against Corporate Social Responsibility," *Wall Street Journal*, August 23, 2010. http://online.wsj.com.

Karnani is associate professor of strategy at the University of Michigan's Stephen M. Ross School of Business.

❝Karnani's argument is based on two faulty premises. First, the reality is that Corporate Social Responsibility—properly planned and practiced—can and does drive profitability. Second, the reality is that with corporate sins and secrets spilling onto computer screens, empowering citizen activists, it is in a company's self-interest to consider the public interest.❞

—Mike Lawrence, "Why Corporate Responsibility Lives (Despite the WSJ Trying to Kill It)," *What Do You Stand For?*, August 27, 2010. www.coneinc.com.

Lawrence is chief reputation officer at Cone, a strategy and communications agency headquartered in Boston.

Bracketed quotes indicate conflicting positions.

* Editor's Note: While the definition of a primary source can be narrowly or broadly defined, for the purposes of Compact Research, a primary source consists of: 1) results of original research presented by an organization or researcher; 2) eyewitness accounts of events, personal experience, or work experience; 3) first-person editorials offering pundits' opinions; 4) government officials presenting political plans and/or policies; 5) representatives of organizations presenting testimony or policy.

❝Corporate America is rapidly recognizing the economic benefits of joining the green movement, the practical challenge of imminent federal carbon cap and trade legislation, and the marketing value in being perceived as 'green.'❞

—Environmental Law Institute, "The Business of Being Green: How Emerging Laws Make Sustainability an Imperative," 2009. www.eli.org.

The Environmental Law Institute works toward shaping the fields of environmental law, policy, and management, domestically and abroad.

❝Before tossing out those sustainability practices and initiatives, it might be wise to first determine the real value of the efforts—especially the possible rewards for staying the course.❞

—A.T. Kearney, *"Green" Winners: The Performance of Sustainability-Focused Companies During the Financial Crisis*, 2009. www.sustaincommworld.com.

A.T. Kearney is a strategic management consulting firm with offices in the United States and 34 other countries.

❝In Europe and Japan, it's just good business and good government. Here in the Americas, greening is a fascinating opportunity, but for many it looks like a dark forest haunted by the demon of reduced profits.❞

—Chris Lowry, "What Do You Mean by Green?," Evolution Green, November 6, 2010. http://evolutiongreen.com.

Lowry, a green specialist who publishes, speaks, and consults on matters related to business, health, and sustainability, is an adviser with Green Enterprise Ontario.

❝For the vast majority of companies, including most small- to- medium-sized businesses, making green choices means doing things differently [than] they have in the past, which owners/operators perceive as risky.❞

—Dennis Cronin, "Is 'Green' Turning Brown? The Green Movement Must Examine Its Future," *Mission Critical*, July/August 2010.

Cronin is principal of Gilbane Building Company in Providence, Rhode Island.

"A significant number of corporate leaders now recognize there to be an opportunity in addressing environment issues and sustainability. Particularly to the extent they can solve their customers' environmental challenges, and in doing so become positioned for business success."

—Dan Esty, interviewed by Joel Makower, "Can 'Green' Still Lead to 'Gold?,'" GreenBiz, April 25, 2011. www.greenbiz.com.

Esty is head of the Connecticut Department of Energy and Environmental Protection and coauthor of *The Green to Gold Business Playbook*.

"Small businesses have been slow to embrace the green movement, for one very good reason: in the beginning, adopting green technologies was an expensive prospect, with very little benefit other than the satisfaction of feeling that you were doing your part to help."

—US Chamber of Commerce Small Business Nation, "What Is Going Green?," 2011. www.uschambersmallbusinessnation.com.

The US Chamber of Commerce Small Business Nation represents 3 million businesses, as well as state and local chambers and industry associations.

"While there is a great concern for the environment, there is a similar recognition that these changes can be made to pay for themselves, and not be just charity by the firm."

—David Ahlstrom and Garry D. Bruton, *International Management: Strategy and Culture in the Emerging World*. Mason, OH: South-Western Cengage Learning, 2010.

Ahlstrom is a business administration professor at the Chinese University of Hong Kong, and Bruton is a professor of management at Texas Christian University's Neeley School of Business.

"Environmentally responsible business practices are quickly becoming a top priority for many businesses, as more realize the financial benefits and competitive advantages that come with it."

—Kelly Spors, "Five Green Business Trends for 2011," Small Business Trends, January 7, 2011. http://smallbiztrends.com.

Spors is a former reporter for the *Wall Street Journal* and is now with Energy Smart, a Minnesota firm that helps businesses save money through energy efficiency.

Facts and Illustrations

Do the Benefits of Going Green Outweigh the Costs?

- In a March 2011 Gallup poll, the majority of Americans surveyed said they supported **environmental protection** but did not view it as a higher priority than a strong economy.

- In an April 2011 report by the Chicago advertising, marketing, and strategy organization Ogilvy & Mather, **77 percent** of American respondents thought it was important to use eco-friendly cleaning products, but only 45 percent actually did; of Chinese respondents, **88 percent** thought it was important, and **63 percent** did.

- Of 1,300 consumers who participated in an October 2010 survey by the market research group Crowd Science, nearly **50 percent** disagreed with the statement, "I don't believe it makes any difference if I shop 'green.'"

- In a June 2010 survey by the public relations firm Gibbs & Soell, only **29 percent** of executives and **16 percent** of consumers thought that a majority of businesses are committed to sustainability.

- According to a March 2010 report by the consumer marketing firm Mintel, **35 percent** of survey respondents would be willing to pay more for environmentally friendly products.

- A study published in 2009 by the strategic consulting firm A.T. Kearney found that companies committed to sustainability had a **15 percent** stronger financial return even in the down economy.

Economic Growth Takes Priority over Environmental Protection

Americans have traditionally placed high value on efforts to protect the environment but priorities appear to have shifted during the global economic crisis that developed in 2008 and 2009. When asked which should be given higher priority—environmental protection or economic growth—poll results show that Americans now place higher priority on economic growth, even if that means the environment suffers to some extent.

With which of these statements about the environment and the economy do you most agree—protection of the environment should be given priority, even at the risk of curbing economic growth (or) economic growth should be given priority, even if the environment suffers to some extent?

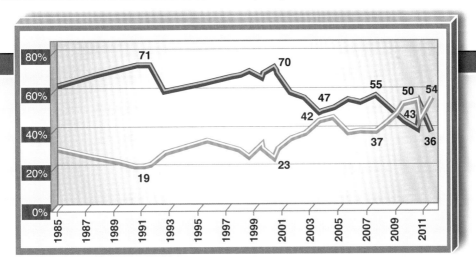

Source: Gallup, "Environment," March 17, 2011. www.gallup.com.

- In an April 2011 Rasmussen Reports survey, **50 percent** of respondents perceived a conflict between economic growth and environmental protection.

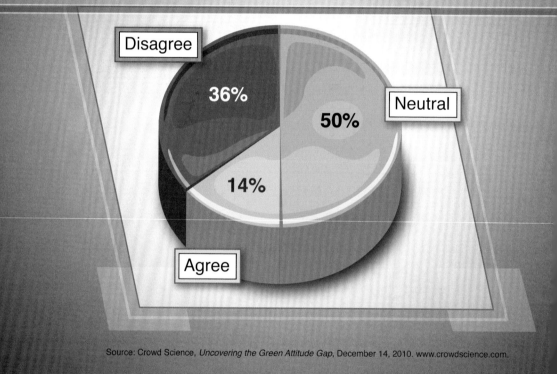

Few Consumers Willing to Spend More for Green Products

Surveys have shown that increasing numbers of consumers are interested in buying products that do not harm the environment. But according to an October 2010 survey by the market research group Crowd Science, only a fraction of consumers are willing to pay substantially more for green products.

I will pay substantially more for products that are better for the environment

Disagree
36%

Neutral
50%

14%

Agree

Source: Crowd Science, *Uncovering the Green Attitude Gap*, December 14, 2010. www.crowdscience.com.

- In a June 2010 survey by the public relations firm Gibbs & Soell, **78 percent** of executives said the primary obstacle to more businesses going green was insufficient return on investment, and **71 percent** said the primary obstacle was consumers' unwillingness to pay a premium for green products and services.

Main Hurdles for Businesses to Go Green

Green movement efforts have played a role in motivating numerous companies to adopt greener business practices. But many executives believe that going green is cost-prohibitive, and are also concerned that consumers are not willing to pay a higher cost for green products or services.

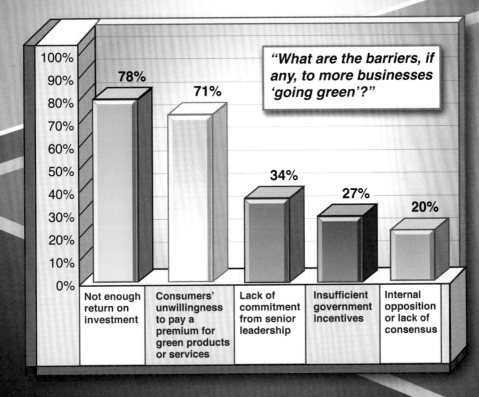

"What are the barriers, if any, to more businesses 'going green'?"

Not enough return on investment	Consumers' unwillingness to pay a premium for green products or services	Lack of commitment from senior leadership	Insufficient government incentives	Internal opposition or lack of consensus
78%	71%	34%	27%	20%

Note: Respondents could choose more than one category.

Source: Gibbs & Soell, *2011 Gibbs & Soell Sense & Sustainability Study*, April 2011. www.gibbs-soell.com.

- According to the Environmental Defense Fund, recycling glass instead of making it from silica (virgin material) reduces mining waste by **70 percent**, water use by **50 percent**, and air pollution by **20 percent**.

What Is the Future of the Green Movement?

“**We need an economy for the twenty-first century, one that is in sync with the earth and its natural support systems, not one that is destroying them.**”

—Lester R. Brown, founder and president of the Earth Policy Institute and former president of Worldwatch Institute.

“**If the environmental movement hopes to be relevant in the future it needs to build a plan for a planet with 8.9 billion people (the projected population in 2050), embrace innovation and technology, and engage corporations as partners in solutions.**”

—Adam Werbach, former president of the Sierra Club and author of *Strategy for Sustainability: A Business Manifesto.*

In recent years the green movement has been the target of criticism for its inability to replicate the immense achievements of the 1970s and 1980s. Even those who are most active in the movement acknowledge that something needs to change in order to again get the public fired up about protecting and preserving the planet. Many say that the answer is youth—getting young people passionate enough about environmental issues that they will become the green leaders of tomorrow. That goal is at the heart of a group called Teens Turning Green, a national student-led environmental advocacy organization. At a conference in Los Angeles that was held in February 2011, the group's founder Judi Shils made a heady statement to an audience of teenagers, telling them: "You are the most powerful people on Earth."[59]

Presenters at the conference emphasized that young people often do not realize how influential they can be in shaping environmental policy. For instance, Renee Sharp, who is a senior scientist and director at the Environmental Working Group, said that legislators do not necessarily expect teens to be passionate about major issues and find it hard to say no when they are face-to-face with young people asking tough questions about environmental protection laws. Jordan Howard, an 18-year-old environmental advocate, expressed that teenagers need to get involved and use their influence to make change happen. "This green movement is a healthy movement," she says. "Once you care about the earth, you begin to care about yourself, and you begin to care about the people that are around you."[60]

Energy for the Future

Since the green movement has existed, energy has been an issue of major importance. Today, the world is heavily dependent on fossil fuels, but these are finite resources that formed over millions of years and will eventually be used up. Although scientists estimate that supplies of these fuels are ample enough to last a few hundred more years (coal is the most plentiful), future energy demands will grow as the world's population continues to increase. Thus, one of the green movement's main focuses for the future is emphasizing new sources of energy such as solar, wind, and geothermal energy.

A lesser known, and virtually untapped, energy source is contained within the earth's oceans. These vast bodies of water cover nearly three-fourths of the planet, and scientists say that their energy potential is im-

> " A lesser known, and virtually untapped, energy source is contained within the earth's oceans. These vast bodies of water cover nearly three-fourths of the planet, and scientists say that their energy potential is immense. "

mense. Daniel Lyons writes in an October 2010 *Newsweek* article that the oceans "seethe and crash around with pent-up energy. What if you could harness that power? As many green venturers have discovered over the years, catching a wave is no easy feat because the oceans are so harsh on equipment and the energy produced is expensive. Now, thanks (ironically) to Big Petroleum, the harvest of the seas is at hand."[61] Lyons says that the technology used in the search for oil and gas buried deep beneath the ocean floor has led to the development of sophisticated new equipment that could potentially harness the energy of ocean waves. This discovery could be the answer to scientists' ability to make use of ocean waves in creating energy, and provide one answer to future energy needs.

A Green Movement Nuke Fan

Nuclear energy has been utilized for years, but the green movement has long fought against it because of the risks involved. The potential dangers of nuclear power became clear in March 2011 after a tsunami struck Japan, crippling a nuclear plant and raising the risk for a radiation disaster in the country. Yet many insist that the problem in Japan was outdated technology in an aging nuclear facility. Nuclear energy, proponents say, is much safer than people think, as well as being a clean source of energy that emits no greenhouses gases into the atmosphere. One of these nuclear power advocates is Stewart Brand, who is considered to be among the "fathers" of the green movement. Like most environmentalists, Brand vehemently opposed nuclear energy in the past, but he has since changed his views.

In his book *Whole Earth Discipline: An Ecopragmatist Manifesto*, Brand argues that technological advancements have made nuclear energy safer than ever before, and he calls for the rapid deployment of a new generation of nuclear power plants. In response to those who are opposed to nuclear power because of the risks, Brand says that this pales in comparison to the damage that is inflicted by burning coal. He writes: "The air pollution from coal burning is estimated to cause 30,000 deaths a year from lung disease in the United States, and 350,000 a year in China. A 1-gigawatt coal plant burns three million tons of fuel a year and produces seven million tons of CO_2, all of which immediately goes into everyone's atmosphere, where no one can control it, and no one knows what it's really up to."[62]

One of the biggest problems with nuclear power is tremendous amounts of radioactive waste. In order for power to be generated, a radioactive heavy metal known as uranium must be enriched, as Lyons explains: "Enrichment is inefficient—some 92 percent of the original uranium gets cast aside as 'depleted uranium.' Worse, once you start enriching uranium to make fuel, you can enrich it further to make material for bombs. But what if you could make nuclear power that didn't need enriched uranium? What about a reactor that runs on depleted uranium?"[63] This was the thinking behind TerraPower, a prototype reactor that has been developed by a Bellevue, Washington, company called Intellectual Ventures.

Nathan Myhrvold, the company's chief executive officer, says that "theoretical calculations and detailed computer simulations" have shown that TerraPower can work. In developing the prototype, the company has consulted with a network of 120 nuclear-power experts, with the goal of getting a test reactor operable by the year 2020. If Myhrvold is correct, nuclear power could provide a solution to the world's increasing demand for clean energy.

> In his book *Whole Earth Discipline: An Ecopragmatist Manifesto,* [Stewart] Brand argues that technological advancements have made nuclear energy safer than ever before, and he calls for the rapid deployment of a new generation of nuclear power plants.

Environmental Health Issues

Annie B. Bond, who is an author and expert on sustainable living, has long been an ardent supporter of green movement efforts. She is disturbed, however, by what she perceives as the tendency of greens to solely focus on harm to the planet such as air and water pollution, waste, and emissions, while at the same time an insidious threat is largely ignored: the toxins that endanger human health. She writes: "The negative toll of toxic chemicals and pollution on our bodies is probably as dramatic as emissions are for the planet, or plastics are for the oceans; the direct link is just harder to make. . . . Many so-called 'green' and 'sustainable' products are simply unhealthy."[64]

Bond cites several examples, such as using recycled tires for children's playgrounds, in which the tires heat up in the sun and emit toxins into the air; energy-saving insulation that seals toxic fumes inside buildings; and cleaning products that are toxic to the lungs. She has a deeply personal reason for wanting toxic chemicals to be a primary green movement focus in the future, as she explains:

> The issue of toxic exposure and its effect on the central nervous system is close to my heart, as 30 years ago I was diagnosed with a clinical, atypical depression, when in fact I had classic organophosphate pesticide poisoning from a pesticide that has since been taken off the market because it was so neurotoxic. I know first hand that exposure to chemicals can be deeply disruptive to the body, causing much suffering.[65]

Numerous companies tout their green packaging and energy-saving efforts and commitment to the environment, but Bond points out that they still sell chemical-laden products. One example is Procter & Gamble, which launched a campaign to help customers use its products in ways that save water, waste, and energy. Bond writes: "P&G appears to be approaching sustainability issues in a way that also doesn't include reducing toxic chemicals in their products. Surely, P&G's initiatives are all good and worthy, but perfectly make my point: What about toxics? How ground-breaking if P&G took a leadership role in reducing non-renewable and toxic chemicals in their products." Bond says that she is issuing an "open invitation" to major corporations to become leaders in reducing toxic chemicals from their products. "In the meantime," she says. "our definition of green needs to broaden to always include health. How ironic that so many so-called 'green' products make us sick."[66]

> " Many in the green movement are aware of the dangers to human health posed by toxic substances. "

Many in the green movement are aware of the dangers to human health posed by toxic substances and have begun taking steps to address this issue. One effort has involved pressuring Congress to pass legislation that would overhaul the Toxic Substances Control Act, which has not been amended since it was passed in 1976 . The Safe Chemicals Act of 2010, which was introduced in April 2010 by US senator Frank Lautenberg, would require safety testing of all industrial chemicals and would expand the EPA's authority to regulate the use of chemicals. In addition, manufacturers would be required to submit proof of the safety of every chemical in production, as well as new chemicals seeking to enter the market. Lautenberg explains: "EPA does not have the tools to act on dangerous chemicals and the chemical industry has asked for stronger laws so that their customers are assured their products are safe. My 'Safe Chemicals Act' will breathe new life into a long-dead statute by empowering EPA to get tough on toxic chemicals."[67]

> " The green movement took the world by storm in 1970, and it has continued to grow larger, stronger, and more influential in the years since. "

Greening Up the Chemical Industry

While it is true that chemicals have a longstanding reputation that is not synonymous with *green*, the chemical industry is working toward greening up its act. For instance, it is responding to the numerous companies that want to reduce or eliminate hazardous substances in order to save money and promote their brands to consumers who demand greener products. Julie Haack, assistant head of the chemistry department at the University of Oregon, explains: "Industry really sees the value of 'green chemistry.' If you want to recruit the best chemists, wouldn't it make sense to promote the opportunity to work in an environment where they can align their interest in the environment with their passion, which is chemistry?"[68]

Universities are getting onboard by creating green chemistry offerings. The University of Oregon, for instance, has started an outreach program that teaches professors about integrating green chemistry into a curriculum. According to Haack, this has increased demand for green chemistry courses throughout the United States, as well as led to changes in how students and faculty approach chemistry. "We've seen subtle shifts," she says. "Instead of students questioning the mechanics of something, now they're thinking about chemistry as a tool for sustainability. They're excited about the possibility of designing out hazards."[69]

In the past, Dow Chemical has not been viewed as a green company, but it is taking steps to change that. For instance, Dow is collaborating with the University of California at Berkeley to create a program that addresses a wide range of issues, from expanding water supplies to measuring the environmental impacts of products' supply chains. In 2008 Dow created the Dow Sustainability Innovation Student Challenge award, which brings together six universities to recognize innovative student projects. Neil Hawkins, Dow Chemical's vice president for sustainability, explains: "If you look at the quality of the projects, you'll see that young people today are on fire to take their skills and know-how and make a difference in the world. As we go out and recruit, to virtually any place on the planet, these issues of sustainability are very important to students."[70]

What Color Will Tomorrow Be?

The green movement took the world by storm in 1970, and it has continued to grow larger, stronger, and more influential in the years since. What the future holds is unknown—but if the past is any indication, the green movement will continue to make strides toward greening the planet and helping people throughout the world live greener, healthier lives. David Walls shares his thoughts: "Reviewing the successes of the last forty years—millions of acres of wilderness saved; air, water, and pesticide pollution reduced; . . . public consciousness raised and powerful organizations built—should give all environmentalists a second wind."[71]

What Is the Future of the Green Movement?

66 As we look to the future, we know what will happen if we fail to create Green Jobs, produce clean and renewable energy, and protect our natural environment. In our nightmares, we can imagine an America with longer unemployment lines, longer gas lines, and rising water lines. 99

—Richard L. Trumka, "Building a Green Collar Movement: Labor and the Environment," speech at the Cornell School of Industrial and Labor Relations, AFL-CIO Media Center, April 9, 2010. www.aflcio.org.

Trumka is president of the AFL-CIO.

66 We need to stop trying to scare the pants off of the American public. Doing so has demonstrably backfired. 99

—Ted Nordhaus and Michael Shellenberger, "The Long Death of Environmentalism," Breakthrough Institute, February 25, 2011. http://thebreakthrough.org.

Nordhaus is a researcher and political strategist, and Shellenberger is president and cofounder of Breakthrough Institute, a conservative public policy think tank.

Bracketed quotes indicate conflicting positions.

* Editor's Note: While the definition of a primary source can be narrowly or broadly defined, for the purposes of Compact Research, a primary source consists of: 1) results of original research presented by an organization or researcher; 2) eyewitness accounts of events, personal experience, or work experience; 3) first-person editorials offering pundits' opinions; 4) government officials presenting political plans and/or policies; 5) representatives of organizations presenting testimony or policy.

> **The future is always difficult to predict, but there are a few key issues on which many people would agree. These issues include the continuing spread of globalization and the importance of international management, . . . greater concern about the environment, and increasing attention given to the poorest populations and regions of the world.**

—David Ahlstrom and Garry D. Bruton, *International Management: Strategy and Culture in the Emerging World*. Mason, OH: South-Western Cengage Learning, 2010.

Ahlstrom is a business administration professor at the Chinese University of Hong Kong, and Bruton is a professor of management at Texas Christian University's Neeley School of Business.

> **The very concept of a green job is not well defined. Is a job still green if it's created not by the market, but by subsidy or mandate?**

—Robert Bryce, "Five Myths About Green Energy," *Washington Post*, April 25, 2010. www.washingtonpost.com.

Bryce is a senior fellow at the Manhattan Institute and the author of *Power Hungry: The Myths of "Green" Energy and the Real Fuels of the Future.*

> **Let me say, as clearly as I can: Every job that produces clean and renewable energy; every job that contributes to the clean and responsible use of energy; and every job that protects our air, our water and our planet—is a Green Job.**

—Richard L. Trumka, "Building a Green Collar Movement: Labor and the Environment," speech at the Cornell School of Industrial and Labor Relations, AFL-CIO Media Center, April 9, 2010. www.aflcio.org.

Trumka is president of the AFL-CIO.

> **As China's economic growth continues, the Chinese environmental movement may be one of the most significant of the coming century.**

—Liam Leonard and John Barry, eds., *Global Ecological Politics*. Bingley, UK: Emerald Group, 2010.

Leonard is with the Institute of Technology in Sligo, Ireland, and Barry is with Queen's University in Belfast, Northern Ireland.

"Amidst the clear failure of governments to lead the way on climate change (or to persuade people of its importance), corporations and businesses are stepping into the leadership vacuum because they see it as a reputational and financial opportunity."

—Graceann Bennett and Freya Williams, "Mainstream Green," *The Red Papers*, Ogilvy & Mather, April 2011. www.ogilvyearth.com.

Bennett is managing partner and director of strategic planning at Chicago's Ogilvy & Mather, and Williams is cofounder and head of strategy at OgilvyEarth.

"This is what I've been getting at for more than a year here: regardless of what is happening to Planet Earth, the green movement does not have coherent and workable solutions."

—Walter Russell Mead, "Top Green Admits: 'We Are Lost!,'" *American Interest*, May 3, 2011. http://blogs.the-american-interest.com.

Mead is senior fellow for US foreign policy at the Council on Foreign Relations and a leading expert on American foreign policy.

"There is no doubt that green issues will increasingly impact the lives of consumers and the business world for some time to come."

—Jeff Rogut, "What the Green Movement Will Mean for Retailers," *Dynamic Business*, March 26, 2009. www.dynamicbusiness.com.au.

Rogut is executive director of the Australian Centre for Retail Studies.

What Is the Future of the Green Movement?

- Of more than 2,300 American adults who participated in a November 2010 Harris Interactive survey, more than **90 percent** at least somewhat agree with the statement "I am concerned about the planet we are leaving behind for future generations."

- The Environmental Protection Agency warns that if humans continue to emit greenhouse gases at or above the current pace, average **global temperature** will increase 3°F to 7°F (16.1°C to 13.9°C) by 2100.

- New York City's Greener Greater Buildings Plan is expected to result in a reduction of carbon dioxide emissions of nearly **5 percent** and reduce citywide energy costs by $700 million annually by 2030.

- A study published in February 2011 by the sustainability consulting firm Ceres found that investments in pollution controls and new generation capacity over five years will create significant numbers of **new jobs**, with the largest estimated job gains in Illinois, Virginia, Tennessee, North Carolina, and Ohio (in that order).

- According to the Environmental Protection Agency, global warming is affecting the stability of the **West Antarctic ice sheet**; the agency warns that a sudden collapse of the ice sheet could raise sea levels 16 to 20 feet (4.88 to 6.01 m).

The Promise of Renewable Energy

One of the primary focuses of green movement efforts has been the expansion of renewable energy sources in order to move away from dependence on fossil fuels, especially coal. Although coal is expected to remain an important fuel source in the coming years, this graph shows the anticipated growth of renewable energy for electricity generation through the year 2035, with wind power having the highest amount of potential.

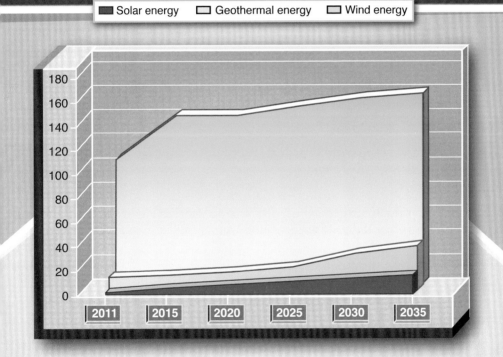

Electricity generation from renewable energy 2011 through 2035 (billion kilowatts per year)

Solar energy   Geothermal energy   Wind energy

Source: US Energy Information Administration, *Annual Energy Outlook 2011*, April 2011. www.eia.gov.

- A study published in October 2009 by scientists from Singapore and Switzerland found that replacing gasoline by converting the world's landfill waste to **biofuel** could cut global carbon emissions by **80 percent**.

Worldwide Perspective on Cause of Climate Change

Of the numerous environmental issues on which the green movement has focused, climate change is among the highest priorities for the future. Many scientists are convinced that the earth is heating at a more rapid rate than should occur naturally. They warn that this is caused by human actions—specifically, the burning of fossil fuels. According to a worldwide Gallup poll conducted in April 2011 residents of most countries share this perspective, although the majority of respondents from the United States believe that climate change is a result of natural causes.

Temperature rise is a part of global warming or climate change. Do you think rising temperatures are . . .

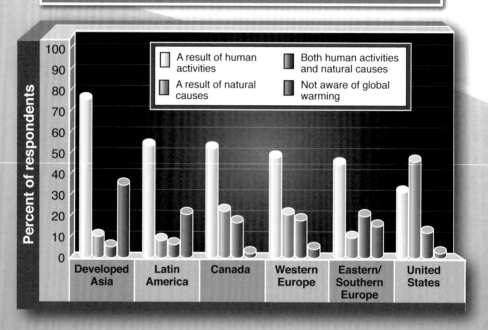

Note: Responses not indicated here were "Don't know/Refused."

Source: Julie Ray and Anita Pugliese, "Worldwide, Blame for Climate Change Falls on Humans," Gallup, April 22, 2011. www.gallup.com.

- A primary green movement goal is to reduce worldwide dependence on fossil fuels (such as coal) for energy production; according to the US Energy Information Administration, electricity demand in the United States alone will increase **41 percent** by 2030.

A Greener Military

Green movement influence has had a significant impact on individuals, businesses, nonprofit groups, and other entities that are taking steps toward achieving a greener future. A study published in April 2010 detailed efforts that the US military is undertaking in order to assume a green leadership position.

Branch of Military	Green Measures Undertaken
US Army	500-megawatt solar power generation plant to help power base at Fort Irwin, California, and end reliance on the public electric grid by 2020; transition to the use of 4,000 electric vehicles, which will save over 100,000 tons of carbon dioxide and cut the use of liquid fossil fuels by 11 million gallons; six pilot projects to demonstrate biomass conversion for fuel use; development of 30-megawatt geothermal project at base in Nevada.
US Navy	Reducing petroleum use in commercial fleet by 50 percent by 2015; launching "Great Green Fleet," a strike group powered completely by alternative fuels by 2016; producing half of all shore-based energy from alternative sources by 2020; ensuring that 50 percent of total energy consumed comes from alternative energy by 2020.
US Air Force	Introduced comprehensive energy program with objective to "make energy a consideration in all that we do"; using flight simulators to save fuel for training purposes; focusing on developing renewable and alternative energy for aviation, ground operation, and installations by meeting 25 percent of base energy needs with renewable energy by 2025 and obtaining 50 percent of aviation fuels from biofuel blends by 2016.
US Marine Corps	Reduce energy consumption 30 percent by 2015; reduce water consumption 16 percent by 2015; increase renewable electric energy by 25 percent by 2025.

Source: Pew Project on National Security, Energy, and Climate, *Reenergizing America's Defense*, April 20, 2010. www.pewtrusts.org.

- In 2010 the Marine Board of the European Science Foundation concluded that by 2050 Europe could draw **50 percent** of its electrical power from the harnessed energy of ocean waves.

Key People and Advocacy Groups

Stewart Brand: An environmental activist who helped spark the green movement during the 1970s and who has become controversial because of his belief that genetically engineered food, nuclear energy, and biotechnology are a necessary part of a green future.

Lester R. Brown: Founder and president of the Earth Policy Institute and former president of Worldwatch Institute.

Robert Bryce: A senior fellow at the Manhattan Institute and the author of *Power Hungry: The Myths of "Green" Energy and the Real Fuels of the Future.*

Rachel Carson: An environmental scientist who wrote the book *Silent Spring,* which became known as a major catalyst for growth of the green movement.

Paul R. Ehrlich: A scientist and environmentalist widely known for being a pioneer in alerting the public to the problems of overpopulation, dwindling resources, and the environment as matters of public policy.

George Perkins Marsh: An attorney and scholar from Vermont who is considered to be America's first environmentalist and who warned of environmental destruction in his 1864 book *Man and Nature; or, Physical Geography as Modified by Human Action.*

Margaret Mead: An American cultural anthropologist and avid environmentalist who actively participated in establishing the International Earth Day tradition at the United Nations.

John Muir: A Scottish-born conservationist and naturalist who founded the Sierra Club in 1892 and served as the organization's president until his death in 1914.

Gaylord Nelson: A US senator from Wisconsin who founded the first Earth Day in 1970.

Sierra Club: One of the oldest, largest, and most influential grassroots environmental organizations in the world.

Alex Steffen: A writer, strategic consultant, and sustainability expert who founded the media organization WorldChanging.

Henry David Thoreau: An American philosopher and naturalist whose essays and books told of his respect of and love for nature and who is known as one of the earliest champions of the environment.

Adam Werbach: The former president of the Sierra Club, noted environmentalist, and author of *Strategy for Sustainability: A Business Manifesto*.

Chronology

1955
The Air Pollution Control Act is passed by Congress, becoming the first piece of legislation to address air pollution in the United States.

1864
Attorney and scholar George Perkins Marsh publishes the book *Man and Nature; or, Physical Geography as Modified by Human Action*, in which he warns of environmental destruction.

1969
US senator Gaylord Nelson authorizes the formation of national "teach-ins" about environmental issues, which leads to the first Earth Day the following year.

1951
The Nature Conservancy is established in Washington, DC, as an organization whose mission is to protect ecologically important lands and waters around the world.

1962
Rachel Carson's book *Silent Spring* is published and becomes known as one of the catalysts for the modern green movement.

1850

1950

1970

1892
The Sierra Club is founded by Scottish-born conservationist and naturalist John Muir, who becomes the grassroots organization's first president.

1952
A governmental group called the Paley Commission releases a report entitled *Resources for Freedom*, which details the United States' increasing dependence on foreign sources of natural resources and argues for the necessity of transitioning to renewable energy.

1956
The Sierra Club gains national recognition for protesting construction of the Echo Park Dam in Dinosaur National Monument in Utah. After extensive lobbying by the group, Congress removes the prospective dam from the Colorado River project.

1946
The Natural Resources Council of America is founded for the purpose of creating partnerships among environmental groups and corporations in the United States.

1968
The crew of the *Apollo 8* moon mission takes the first photograph of Earth from space, and it becomes the iconic image of the green movement.

1970

President Richard Nixon signs the National Environmental Policy Act into law, providing the foundation for wide-reaching environmental policy. This same year the Environmental Protection Agency, the Natural Resources Defense Council, and the National Oceanographic and Atmospheric Administration are established.

2011

In a major victory against greenwashing, a settlement by the US Federal Trade Commission stops deceptive tactics by Tested Green, a company that issued hundreds of bogus environmental certifications of products.

1972

The pesticide DDT is banned in the United States, the result of nearly 10 years of legislative battles that followed revelations in Rachel Carson's book *Silent Spring*.

2009

A documentary film called *Earth Days*, which chronicles the environmental movement in the United States, is released by independent film distributor Zeitgeist Films.

1970

2000

1987

The United Nations publishes a report entitled *Our Common Future*, which documents global problems of poverty, expanding population, resource scarcity, and deterioration of oceans and forests.

2004

Breakthrough Institute president Michael Shellenberger and political strategist Ted Nordhaus release a report called *The Death of Environmentalism*, which suggests that the modern green movement is not capable of dealing with the world's most serious environmental problems.

2010

An estimated 1 billion people worldwide pay tribute to 40 years of green movement accomplishments by celebrating the anniversary of Earth Day.

2006

Former vice president Al Gore releases *An Inconvenient Truth*, a documentary film intended to educate the public about the dangers of global warming to the planet.

1988

National Aeronautics and Space Administration (NASA) scientist James Hansen warns Congress about the consequences of global warming, leading to the formation of the Intergovernmental Panel on Climate Change (IPCC).

2005

In the case *Rapanos v. United States*, the US Supreme Court rules that the Clean Air Act only pertains to "relatively permanent, standing or flowing bodies of water" and does not protect wetlands.

Related Organizations

Breakthrough Institute

436 14th St., Suite 820
Oakland, CA 94612
phone: (510) 550-8800
e-mail: michael@thebreakthrough.org
website: www.thebreakthrough.org

The Breakthrough Institute is a conservative public policy think tank located in Oakland, California. A number of articles and reports are available on its website on topics such as technology, energy consumption, climate change, and environmental policy.

Cato Institute

1000 Massachusetts Ave. NW
Washington, DC 20001
phone: (202) 842-0200 • fax: (202) 842-3490
e-mail: cato@cato.org • website: www.cato.org

The Cato Institute is a public policy research organization that is dedicated to the principles of liberty, limited government, and free markets. Its website offers a variety of publications, a "research areas" section, newsletters, podcasts, and a search engine that produces a number of articles on issues related to the green movement.

Earth Day Network

1616 P St. NW, Suite 340
Washington, DC 20036
phone: (202) 518-0044
e-mail: info@earthday.org • website: www.earthday.org

Earth Day Network seeks to broaden, diversify, and activate the environmental movement worldwide through a combination of education, public policy, and consumer campaigns. Its website features news articles, a photo gallery, a link to a blog, and a special section on how the organization has helped influence environmental policy.

Environmental Literacy Council

1625 K St. NW, Suite 1020
Washington, DC 20006
phone: (202) 296-0390 • fax: (202) 822-0991
e-mail: info@enviroliteracy.org • website: www.enviroliteracy.org

Composed of scientists, economists, and educators, the Environmental Literacy Council offers free information about environmental science to educators, students, policy makers, and the public. An extensive variety of publications are available on its website on such issues as climate, water, ecosystems, energy, and environment and society.

Green Youth Movement

PO Box 10485
Beverly Hills, CA 90213
phone: (310) 888-3367
e-mail: info@greenyouthmovement.org
website: www.greenyouthmovement.org

Founded by Los Angeles teenager Ally Maize, the Green Youth Movement seeks to educate children and teenagers about environmental awareness, eco-friendly behavior, and the small steps that collectively can make a difference for the future. Its website offers news articles, videoclips, special sections for kids and teens, and tips for greener living.

International Institute for Sustainable Development

161 Portage Ave. East, 6th Floor
Winnipeg, MB R3B 0Y4 Canada
phone: (204) 958-7700 • fax: (204) 958-7710
e-mail: info@iisd.ca • website: www.iisd.org

The International Institute for Sustainable Development is a public policy research institute that has a long history of conducting research into sustainable development. Its website offers numerous publications on sustainability-related issues, archived news releases, a sustainable development timeline, current initiatives, and a number of reports.

National Center for Policy Analysis

12770 Coit Rd., Suite 800
Dallas, TX 75251
phone: (972) 386-6272
website: www.ncpa.org

A conservative organization that advocates private, free-market alternatives to government regulation and control, the National Center for Policy Analysis views many environmental policies as misguided efforts. Its website has an environmental section that produces numerous articles and commentaries on environmental reform, global warming, and energy in the future.

Natural Resources Defense Council

40 West 20th St.
New York, NY 10011
phone: (212) 727-2700 • fax: (212) 727-1773
e-mail: nrdcinfo@nrdc.org • website: www.nrdc.org

The Natural Resources Defense Council is an environmental action organization that works to ensure a safe and healthy environment for all living things. Its website offers a wealth of information including Smarter Living and Smarter Business sections, news articles, *OnEarth* and *Nature's Voice* magazines, current issues, and NRDC-TV videos.

Nature Conservancy

4245 North Fairfax Dr., Suite 100
Arlington, VA 22203
phone: (703) 841-5300 • fax: (703) 841-1283
website: www.nature.org

The Nature Conservancy works to protect the environment on behalf of people and nature in order to achieve a sustainable world. Its website offers news releases, inspirational stories, information about current initiatives, a search engine that produces articles about environmental issues, and a link to the *Cool Green Science* blog.

Sierra Club

85 Second St., 2nd Floor
San Francisco, CA 94105
phone: (415) 977-5500 • fax: (415) 977-5799
e-mail: information@sierraclub.org • website: www.sierraclub.org

The Sierra Club works to protect communities, wild places, and the planet itself. Its website offers the *Sierra Club Insider* newsletter, *Sierra Magazine*, and extensive information about issues such as clean energy and transportation, emissions, global warming, and other priorities. Also available through the site is a link to the Sierra Student Coalition website.

Teens Turning Green

2330 Marinship Way, Suite 370
Sausalito, CA 94965
phone: (415) 289-1001
e-mail: judi@teensturninggreen.org
website: www.teensturninggreen.org

Teens Turning Green is a student-led movement devoted to education and advocacy for environmentally and socially responsible choices for individuals, schools, and communities. Its website offers news articles, links to videos and a blog, and information about current programs and activities.

US Environmental Protection Agency (EPA)

Ariel Rios Bldg.
1200 Pennsylvania Ave. NW
Washington, DC 20004
phone: (202) 272-0167
e-mail: info@epa.gov • website: www.epa.gov

The EPA's mission is to protect human health and the environment. Its website features news releases, research topics, a "Science and Technology" section, a link to the *Greenversations* blog, and a search engine that produces a variety of articles on environmental issues.

For Further Research

Books

Stewart Brand, *Whole Earth Discipline*: *An Ecopragmatist Manifesto*. New York: Viking, 2009.

E—The Environmental Magazine, Earth Talk: Expert Answers to Everyday Questions About the Environment. New York: Plume, 2009.

Jennifer Fosket and Laura Mamo, *Living Green: Communities That Sustain*. Gabriola Island, BC: New Society, 2009.

Benjamin Kline, *First Along the River: A Brief History of the U.S. Environmental Movement*. Lanham, MD: Rowman & Littlefield, 2011.

Aric McBay, Lierre Keith, and Derrick Jensen, *Deep Green Resistance: Strategy to Save the Planet*. New York: Seven Stories, 2011.

Carol McClelland, *Green Careers for Dummies*. Hoboken, NJ: Wiley, 2010.

Sandy Moore and Deanna Moore, *The Green Intention: Living in Sustainable Joy*. Camarillo, CA: DeVorss, 2010.

Sharon J. Smith, *The Young Activist's Guide to Building a Green Movement + Changing the World*. Berkeley, CA: Ten Speed, 2011.

Alex Steffen, ed., *Worldchanging: A User's Guide for the 21st Century*. New York: Abrams, 2011.

Periodicals

Dennis Cronin, "Is 'Green' Turning Brown? The Green Movement Must Examine Its Future," *Mission Critical*, July/August 2010.

Jenny Deam, "Pedal Power: An Old-Fashioned Concept Makes a Modern Comeback to Help Save the Planet and Keep Kids Healthy, *Kiwi Magazine*, August/September 2010.

Kate Galbraith, "Coverage of Green Issues Becomes More Specialized," *New York Times*, February 20, 2011.

Jeff Goodell, "Q&A: Bill Gates on How to Stop Global Warming," *Rolling Stone*, October 28, 2010.

Aneel Karnani, "The Case Against Corporate Social Responsibility," *Wall Street Journal*, August 23, 2010.

Daniel Lyons, "10 Big Green Ideas," *Newsweek*, October 18, 2010.

Jason Mark, "Talkin' 'Bout My Generation: Can a New Group of Young Environmental Leaders Reinvigorate Green's Grassroots Spirit?," *Earth Island Journal*, Winter 2011.

Jack Neff, "Earth Day at 40: Where Do We Stand?," *Waste & Recycling News*, April 26, 2010.

Ted Nordhaus and Michael Shellenberger, "The Green Bubble," *New Republic*, May 20, 2009.

Bradford Plumer, "Eco-Movement Faces a Hostile Climate," *New Republic*, April 21, 2011.

San Diego Union-Tribune, "The Green Economy," April 17, 2011.

John Sullivan, "'Greenwashing' Gets His Goat: Environmental Activist Coined Famous Term," *Times Herald-Record*, August 1, 2009.

Bryan Walsh, "Has Environmentalism Lost Its Spiritual Core?," *Time*, December 6, 2010.

Internet Sources

Graceann Bennett and Freya Williams, "Mainstream Green," *The Red Papers*: Ogilvy & Mather, April 2011. http://assets.ogilvy.com/truffles_email/ogilvyearth/Mainstream_Green.pdf.

Ursula M. Burns, "Is the Green Movement a Passing Fancy?," *Bloomberg Businessweek*, January 27, 2009. www.businessweek.com/technology/content/jan2009/tc20090126_136438.htm.

Alex Steffen, "Bright Green, Light Green, Dark Green, Gray: The New Environmental Spectrum," Worldchanging, February 27, 2009. www.worldchanging.com/archives/009499.html.

Rebecca Tarbotton, "Has Earth Day Become Corporate Greenwash Day?," *Huffington Post*, April 22, 2010. www.huffingtonpost.com/rebecca-tarbotton/has-earth-day-become-corp_b_548066.html.

TerraChoice, *The Sins of Greenwashing*, 2010. http://sinsofgreenwashing.org/findings/greenwashing-report-2010.

Source Notes

Overview

1. Gaylord Nelson, "Earth Day '70: What It Meant," Environmental Protection Agency History, April 1980. www.epa.gov.
2. Wangari Maathai, *Replenishing the Earth: Spiritual Values for Healing Ourselves and the World.* New York: Doubleday, 2010.
3. Quoted in PBS, "The National Parks: America's Best Idea," 2009. www.pbs.org.
4. David Walls, "Environmental Movement," Sonoma State University, May 11, 2008. www.sonoma.edu.
5. Sierra Club, "Gift Planning: Rachel Carson Society," 2011. www.sierraclub.org.
6. Walls, "Environmental Movement."
7. Center for Sustainability at Aquinas College, "What Is Sustainability?" www.centerforsustainability.org.
8. Bryan Walsh, "Has Environmentalism Lost Its Spiritual Core?," *Time,* December 6, 2010. www.time.com.
9. Tom Burack, "There Are Many Shades of Green," news release, New Hampshire Department of Environmental Services, April 20, 2010. http://des.nh.gov.
10. Quoted in Olivia Fermi, "Making Vancouver Sustainable: Greenest City Meets Village Vancouver," *Vancouver Observer,* March 7, 2011. www.vancouverobserver.com.
11. Erika Parker, "Five Companies You Can Trust Are Going Green," *Going Green Today,* March 4, 2011. www.goinggreentoday.com.
12. Mike Kapalko, "Greenwashing: Making Companies Come Clean About Their Claims," *Sustainability,* Winter 2010. www.cmmonline.com.
13. TerraChoice, *The Sins of Greenwashing: Home and Family Edition,* October 2010. http://sinsofgreenwashing.org.
14. Bryan Walsh, "Foodies Can Eclipse (and Save) the Green Movement," *Time,* February 15, 2011. www.time.com.
15. Jason Mark, "Talkin' 'Bout My Generation: Can a New Group of Environmental Leaders Reinvigorate Green's Grassroots Spirit?," *Earth Island Journal,* p. 42.
16. Larry West, "When Did the U.S. Environmental Movement Begin?," About.com Environmental Issues, 2011. http://environment.about.com.

What Is the Green Movement?

17. Ally Maize, "Ally's Story," Green Youth Movement, 2009. www.greenyouthmovement.org.
18. Quoted in Joel Leyden, "Ally Maize's Green Youth Movement—Changing the World 'One Kid at a Time,'" Rochelle and Richard Maize Foundation blog, March 24, 2010. http://richardmaize1.blogspot.com.
19. Peter Senge, interview by Michael S. Hopkins, "Sustainability: Not What You Think It Is," *MIT Sloan Management Review,* June 2009. http://sloanreview.mit.edu.
20. Quoted in Senge, "Sustainability: Not What You Think It Is."
21. Senge, "Sustainability: Not What You Think It Is."
22. Alice Marcus Krieg, e-mail interview with author, May 19, 2011.
23. Marcus Krieg, e-mail interview with author.

24. Natural Resources Defense Council, "New York, New York: 2010 Smarter City—Energy," July 16, 2010. http://smartercities.nrdc.org.

25. National Sustainable Agriculture Coalition, "Conservation, Energy & Environment," 2010. http://sustainableagriculture.net.

26. Walsh, "Foodies Can Eclipse (and Save) the Green Movement."

27. Michael Pollan, "The Food Movement, Rising," *New York Review of Books*, June 10, 2010. www.nybooks.com.

28. Quoted in Laura Fraser, "Kicking the Chemical Habit," *Onearth*, April 26, 2011. www.onearth.org.

29. Jim Cochran, "When It Comes to Food, One Size Doesn't Fit All," *Onearth*, April 28, 2011. www.onearth.org.

30. Anti-Defamation League Law Enforcement Agency Resource Network, "Ecoterrorism: Extremism in the Animal Rights and Environmentalism Movements." www.adl.org.

31. Anti-Defamation League Law Enforcement Agency Resource Network, "Ecoterrorism."

How Has the Green Movement Influenced Environmental Policies?

32. Quoted in Christopher Maag, "From the Ashes of '69, a River Reborn," *New York Times*, June 21, 2009. www.nytimes.com.

33. National Park Service, *Cuyahoga River Recovers*, 2009. www.nps.gov.

34. Nelson, "Earth Day '70: What It Meant."

35. Jack Lewis, "The Birth of EPA," *EPA Journal*, November 1985. www.epa.gov.

36. Quoted in David Kirby, "Made in China: Our Toxic, Imported Air Pollution," *Discover Magazine*, March 18, 2011. http://discovermagazine.com.

37. Quoted in Sierra Club, "Community Members, Environmental Groups Praise Legislative Effort to Kick Coal Out of Massachusetts," May 18, 2011. http://www.sierraclub.org.

38. Quoted in Michelle Frey, "Greenpeace Activists Climb Deadly Smokestack at Fisk Coal Plant in Chicago," Greenpeace, May 24, 2011. www.greenpeace.org.

39. Bill Gates, interview by Jeff Goodell, "Q&A: Bill Gates on How to Stop Global Warming," *Rolling Stone*, October 28, 2010. www.rollingstone.com.

40. Bradford Plumer, "Eco-Movement Faces a Hostile Climate," *New Republic*, April 21, 2011. www.tnr.org.

41. Plumer, "Eco-Movement Faces a Hostile Climate."

42. Plumer, "Eco-Movement Faces a Hostile Climate."

Do the Benefits of Going Green Outweigh the Costs?

43. Ursula M. Burns, "Is the Green Movement a Passing Fancy?," *Bloomberg Businessweek*, January 27, 2009. www.businessweek.com.

44. Burns, "Is the Green Movement a Passing Fancy?"

45. Burns, "Is the Green Movement a Passing Fancy?"

46. Aneel Karnani, "The Case Against Social Responsibility," *Wall Street Journal*, August 23, 2010. http://online.wsj.com.

47. Karnani, "The Case Against Social Responsibility."

48. Karnani, "The Case Against Social Responsibility."

49. Quoted in Jim Motavilli, "A History of Greenwashing: How Dirty Towels Impacted the Green Movement," WalletPop, February 12, 2011. www.walletpop.com.

50. Quoted in Motavilli, "A History of Greenwashing."

51. Quoted in Tiffany Hsu, "Skepticism Grows over Products Touted as Eco-Friendly," *Los Angeles Times*, May 21, 2011. www.latimes.com.

52. Quoted in Michelle J. Katz, "FTC Settlement Ends 'Tested Green' Certifications That Were Neither Tested Nor Green," Federal Trade Commission, news release, January 11, 2011. www.ftc.gov.

53. Graceann Bennett and Freya Williams, "Mainstream Green," *The Red Papers*, Ogilvy & Mather, April 2011. www.ogilvyearth.com.

54. Derrick Jensen, "Forget Shorter Showers," *Orion Magazine*, July/August 2009. www.orionmagazine.org.

55. Jensen, "Forget Shorter Showers."

56. Quoted in Jensen, "Forget Shorter Showers."

57. Bennett and Williams, "Mainstream Green."

58. Joel Makower, "Why Doesn't Green = Better?," Two Steps Forward, July 2009. http://makower.typepad.com.

What Is the Future of the Green Movement?

59. Quoted in Raquel Estupinan, "Environmental Conference Urges Teens to Turn 'Green,'" *South Los Angeles Report*, February 28, 2011. www.intersectionssouthla.org.

60. Quoted in Estupinan, "Environmental Conference Urges Teens to Turn 'Green.'"

61. Daniel Lyons, "10 Big Green Ideas," *Newsweek*, October 18, 2010. www.newsweek.com.

62. Quoted in Todd Woody, "Stewart Brand's Strange Trip: Whole Earth to Nuclear Power," *Yale Environment 360*, December 22, 2009. http://e360.yale.edu.

63. Lyons, "10 Big Green Ideas."

64. Annie B. Bond, "Why the Green Movement Should Include Environmental Health Issues," *Huffington Post*, April 22, 2010. www.huffingtonpost.com.

65. Bond, "Why the Green Movement Should Include Environmental Health Issues."

66. Bond, "Why the Green Movement Should Include Environmental Health Issues."

67. Frank Lautenberg, "Lautenberg Introduces 'Safe Chemicals Act' to Protect Americans from Toxic Chemicals," April 15, 2010. http://lautenberg.senate.gov.

68. Quoted in Sara Goodman, "'Green Chemistry' Movement Sprouts in Colleges, Companies," *New York Times*, March 25, 2009. www.nytimes.com.

69. Quoted in Goodman, "'Green Chemistry' Movement Sprouts in Colleges, Companies."

70. Quoted in Goodman, "'Green Chemistry' Movement Sprouts in Colleges, Companies."

71. Walls, "Environmental Movement."

List of Illustrations

Index

Index

About the Author

Peggy J. Parks holds a bachelor of science degree from Aquinas College in Grand Rapids, Michigan, where she graduated magna cum laude. An author who has written over 100 educational books for children and young adults, Parks lives in Muskegon, Michigan, a town that she says inspires her writing because of its location on the shores of Lake Michigan.